TWO PLAYS

A MOST UNSUITABLE GIRL

and

CONQUEST AT NOON

TWO PLAYS

A MOST UNSUITABLE GIRL

A Play on Dowry Deaths

and

CONQUEST AT NOON

A Historical Fantasy

Rajesh Talwar

KALPAZ PUBLICATIONS

Delhi-110 052

TWO PLAYS
A MOST UNSUITABLE GIRL
and
CONQUEST AT NOON
(Literature)

ISBN: 81-7835-110-2

Published in 2003 in India by
Kalpaz Publications
C-30, Satyawati Nagar
Delhi-110052
E-mail : Kalpaz@hotmail.com
Visit our website at : www.gyanbooks.com

Lasertypesetting by: Varsha Graphics, Delhi
Printed by: Chawla Offset Press, Delhi

Dedication

for

Nitya Ramakrishnan

Preface to 'A Most Unsuitable Girl'

It was my impression when I circulated amongst friends a shorter version of this play that a preface to 'A Most Unsuitable Girl' was not really required, so I thought that I would try, in the manner of formal public speakers on festive occasions to keep it as it as brief as possible. My author's feeling about this particular play was that it was in danger of being over-discussed by me, with inimical consequences for potential readers.

The reaction of some of my friends who saw the 'preview' as it were compelled me to change this decision and to expand the play to its present length.

Reactions were varied. The plot appealed to someone like Ayeesha Karim, a lawyer-friend (this species is very rare) in Delhi, now practising law in Jordan, who specialised in dealing with cases of dowry deaths. To my pleasurable amazement, the story struck a powerful chord in her; and she avidly pounced upon the idea of the sexual jealousy of mothers in law playing a much ignored but extremely significant role in the carrying out of these unspeakably bestial crimes.

On the other hand a Swiss friend, Yves del Monaco, did not quite comprehend the necessity or relevance of the introductory scene and the very last one, which show a judge, a prosecutor and a defence counsel talking shop and analysing the tale of this attempted dowry killing.

At the risk of digressing somewhat let me explain that this part of the play's structure is there really to indicate how the judiciary is not really in any exalted position, separated from the morality of the masses. Thus the puritan judge, who views Poonam's somewhat extravagant sexuality are denoting 'characterlessness' is possibly more biased and socially prejudiced than the blue movie watching prosecutor.

I am reminded here of a short by Oscar Wilde, that merciless critic of social hypocrisies, in which a tortoise tells a water rat, the story of the exploitation of Hans, a trusting soul, by his best friend. This story is told of the various acts by which Hans is gradually stripped of all his property and assets, by this 'friend'. What makes the story stand out is that the water rat comprehends the story not from Hans point of view, or from the point of view of an unbiased observer, but instead *from the pretending friends point of view.* In other words a villain's point of view, and herein lies the significance of the listener being a 'water rat'.* In this play too, in the last scene, the reactions of the legal fraternity are mixed, more complex certainly than that of a water rat, but nevertheless imbued partially with the prejudices that make dowry deaths occur.

Other reasons for having the opening and closing scenes of the play performed mainly by Courtroom characters. It would introduce some distancing, which may be an advantage in a play that seeks to induce some audience reflection. This device also permits me to introduce differing perspectives on dowry deaths, which reflect perspectives prevalent in mainstream Indian society.

The court functionaries also discuss some legal angles, which are not without interest.

The play has been written in English, but an attempt has been made to indianize the language in terms of vocabulary, speech patterns, and even frequent use of colloquial expressions and exclamations in order to correspond better with how English is spoken by many Indians. The aim is to make the play more authentic and the characters more believable.

This play itself is not a tragedy. If anything it purports (sic) to be a comedy. When Joseph Heller planned on writing 'Catch 22', someone questioned him as to whether it was even possible to write a comedy on an event as terrible and tragic as World

---

* In the very end of this story, as I recall it, the tortoise after telling his tale is startled at how the water rat receives the story—as validation of the villain's point of view! 'But don't you understand the moral of the story', he pleads. 'You mean you dared to tell me a story with a moral?' accuses the water rat, and walks away disgustedly.

War II. That he did in fact do so, with incredible success, is in itself a part answer to the question posed.

('A comedy about dowry deaths!' I was similarly queried. 'You must be joking!')

In fact a serious play on such an issue is in danger of becoming didactic.

It is Poonam's character in fact that prevents the possibility of didacticism. Had she been a stereotypical virginal, unreal beauty of the kind shown in Bollywood her brutal oppression and exploitation at the hands of her in-laws would have made the story line didactic and even worse entirely predictable.

At a last word, I do hope (with some self indulgence perhaps) that his particular comedy too will not prove any less effective in dealing with the issue of dowry deaths as compared with other tragic plays written on the subject.

Preface to Conquest at Noon

This play, unlike the previous one, does require an introduction.

The idea of writing it came to me in the summer of 2000, after I had been chosen for an assignment with the UN in the capacity of a legal officer at Kosovo.

On the flight from New Delhi to Frankfurt, and thereafter to Munich and Skopje, capital of Macedonia I happened to re-read 'The Autobiography of Malcolm X'. Throughout the powerful discourse in the book, the protagonist Malcolm uses crude racial categories of white, black, brown and yellow. Did Malcolm X preach reverse racism for most of his life? Or did he merely endeavor to startle people out of their complacent, conditioned mindsets by deliberately making provocative statements and arguments..

During the drive from Skopje to Pristina in the UN vehicle, which had been sent to pick me up, I saw heaps of UN vehicles and those belonging to innumerable charitable organizations lined up at the checkpoint. In the weeks that followed I would witness first hand how the UN for the first time in the recorded history of the organization was actually administering and governing a territory.

The UNMIK (United Nations Interim Mission in Kosovo) comprised a large multinational presence in which were included very many Africans and Asians. Within the civilian police for instance (or CIVPOL as it is called in UN terminology) were employed several hundred policemen from India, Pakistan and Bangladesh. Hardly three months prior to my arrival, there had arrived on a chartered flight from New Delhi three hundred policemen from various parts of India, to augment the existing police force already comprising of very many Indians.

During my first days in Pristina, when I was lodged at the UNMIK hotel one morning at breakfast one of my UN compatriots Jutta, a fresh arrival from Germany remarked to me in the context of the multinational police force how strange it must feel for an Albanian, who commits say a traffic violation, to be descended upon by a black, brown, yellow and white assortment of nationalities.

It seemed neo-colonial to Jutta – this benevolent administration by a multinational UN force. What struck me however was that a white population – neither the Albanian Muslims nor the Serbs can be distinguished in terms of physical characteristics from Europeans - was being administered, governed, *ruled* by a (partly) brown, black and yellow administration.

In the recent history of the African and Asian people – that recent history, which can be remembered, identified with – there are few, if any instances where a white people were subjugated by them. Sure, Chenghez Khan and his hordes (sic) subjugated millions of whites in Central Asia and beyond, but that happened more than a thousand years ago. Similarly the Arab expansion in the century included various territories in Europe, but this was 'a long time ago'. These are not events the current, living generation can easily identify with as they seem to belong to a remote, inaccessible past. It is not something, for instance, that we read in the newspapers while growing up, or watched on telly as a child.

This fact of history – the fact that in recent times it is only the black, yellow or brown race which has been at the receiving end – this fact by itself perpetuates racism, even after the particular chapters of colonization have been concluded.

How does this happen? It happens in two ways. It happens firstly because it convinces some (though not all) of the whites of their inherent superiority over other races. 'We've been ruling these other races all over the globe,' he tells himself. 'Doesn't that mean that we are superior?'

The other way this fact operates is to convince Asians, Africans and Latinos that they are actually inferior. 'I could say my culture is greater,' he thinks, 'but of what use was that great culture of mine? Was it even great, if it couldn't prevent our eventual enslavement and subjugation?'

Racism is thus perpetuated through beliefs of superiority and inferiority.

The former colonized subject could of course have reacted differently. He could for instance have said, 'My culture is great, *even though* I was enslaved and subjugated.' Nationalists and patriots from newly independent countries have frequently articulated such responses, but *despite their truth,* somewhere in the minds of the defeated people they sound hysterical and ring hollow. When Tagore phrased such like arguments before the Japanese in 1941, he was sneered at!

The loss of confidence in one's own culture subsequent to military defeat and vanquishment seems irremediable. Perhaps it is only when economic resurgence takes place in formerly colonized societies that there will come into being a renewed pride in their traditions, systems of medicine, religion, way of life, culture, etc.

Great literature from Asia, Africa and Latin America has already addressed such issues. It may be that my reading is somewhere deficient, but I believe that there have been few dramatic works – and plays can sometimes have a mass appeal not available to more esoteric literary devices – which have dealt with these matters.

The play is a sincere and humble attempt to address large and complex issues. It evidently uses racial categories, as in Malcolm X's book, but the purpose in writing it is avowedly anti-racist.

Such plays are difficult to write for the reason that they can easily degenerate into some kind of crude reverse propaganda and empty lectures merely sounding off homilies known to everyone.

As part insurance against any such mishap, but largely

for my own very great pleasure, I have enjoyed playing around with historical dates, places and figures, and including in the last named category a few iconic figures from Indian history and the independence movement as well as lesser, sometimes unsavory personages from more recent times. It is my fervent hope that the net result is an engaging, if not engrossing product. A critic might accuse me of trivializing history and personages. Historical plays are often ponderous and pompous, and this play would represent a change from that species as I have attempted lightness in the play. In self-defense I would argue with my hypothetical critic that it is far better for a playwright to ponder without being ponderous.

Should I write the play in English or in Hindi? This was an important decision I needed to make at the start of my project, as the language question was connected with the subject matter of the play, more so than other plays in a multinational setting.

In an ideal situation, the Bharatian characters should have spoken Hindi (or Hindustani) and the Blitz characters English, but this would have restricted the audience to individuals who spoke and understood both languages ie only metropolitan North India. The original script had to be in one language, and if needed be translated later.

If I choose Hindi, the Blitz characters would appear somewhat fake, yet with English the Bharatian characters would suffer. As English is now undoubtedly the major global language and almost a 'mother tongue' with me (as is the case with millions of urban educated Indians) it seemed to be the obvious and better choice.

As a matter of fact, in order to truly invert history, we would need a completely different language. Languages themselves, be they English, Hindi, German or any other tongue are indelibly imbued with a specific historicity, literally at every turn of phrase.

English having been decided upon then, a second related question was the kind of English the play's characters would speak. Since this was a historical fantasy dating back to events only a few centuries old (sic) it was easy to choose a kind of 'proper' English with characters such as Birchbill, Behru and JP who existed in an earlier period, but with the modern versions of Chanakaya, Socrates and the Princess, it was a question whether or not to spice up their speech with the use of modern slang and colloquial expressions. This has in fact been done in part, despite the consequent absurdity. The false, but inevitable assumption, you see, is that English is a Bharatian language -as well as the language in Blighty.[1] I ask viewers and readers to bear with this absurdity as and when it appears.

In my earlier play, INSIDE GAYLAND, important issues were sought to be examined by imagining a reversed scenario in which on a certain pink planet homosexuality is the norm and heterosexuality criminalized. I enjoyed writing that play very much and a near reversal of homophobic attitudes (to 'heterophobia') did much to spice up the play. In CONQUEST AT NOON on the other hand my playwright's instinct suggested to me that this was not desirable or even realistically possible since the play was written in English, with most Bharatian characters speaking reasonably good English. Had a near reversal been attempted it would have negatively affected the flow of the text, the story would have lost plausibility and most unfortunately of all it would have reinforced stereotypes. There has been consequently been a planned and deliberate blurring and dilution of cultural identity. To my mind this was perfectly appropriate, for while retaining a sense of cultural distinctness, at the same time stereotyping is avoided.

A word about the naming game in this inverted history play. England first became Lingland, but this name was subsequently rejected because of derogatory references that might exist in the Indian, though not in this instance in the English mind. While the play was being written, one day a friend remarked about how the English colonizers in India, spoke nostalgically of going back to 'Blighty.'[2] So Blighty it became, and the residents would logically have the Blits (like the Brits) but in a naming twist they are called the Blitz.

---

1 One could of course argue with reason that this is actually no longer a false assumption (and even if false, will become less and less so, with the passage of time), English is today indeed an Indian language as well.

2. The name has linguistic connections with the similar sounding Urdu or Hindustani word 'vilaity' which meant foreign or foreigner. Blighty was the British soldiers inevitable corruption of it (Source: *Hobson Johnson Anglo Indian Directory*), and came into common use as a term for Britain around the First World War.

And the militant organization in Blighty is called the Blitz Krieg!

The original substitute name I had for India was Bindialand (invoking the similar sounding 'bindia', the traditional round ornament worn by Indian women on their forehead, as an indication of matrimony, or even sometimes fashion nowadays, with young unmarried girls.) This was ultimately abandoned in favor of Maha Bharat, from the great Hindu epic, which translates into Maha or Great Bharat, invoking the idea of a great colonizing power, with obvious similarities to Great Britian. The capital became Indra Prastha[3], and Blighty's capital became simply Tundun.[4] A few names, that do not crop up too frequently are not changed and remain the same, such as Diwan-I-Khas, Thames, etc. The reason for this is that the play assumes a fantastic history for only a few centuries. History prior to this is assumed to be the same.

The inversion of historical personalities is inevitably somewhat blurred and has also deliberately been played around with. Thus it is Clementine, Birchbill's wife who has the affair with Behru, the Prime Minister of Maha Bharat. Lady Mohabattein, (standing in for Lady Mountbatten) is merely Clementine's friend and adviser. An important 'missing person' in the play is Mohandas Karamchand Gandhi for the obvious reason that his humbleness, simplicity and sartorial tastes among other things made it too daunting a task to portray him as a colonizer and empire builder. By contrast it was not so difficult a task to invert Churchill and dress him, so to speak, in the garb of a moderate revolutionary seeking independence for Blighty.

A brief summary of the story line. In the play, Socrates a white man from Blighty (former colony of the great or *Maha*

---

3. In *Mahabharat* the great epic, the sons of Panda build a new capital near Delhi and call it Indraprastha, the supposed ruins of which are still pointed out to the curious traveler.
4. Another interesting phonetic similarity exists between the English word 'abode' and 'abadi', which is a sattlement, and numerous Indian towns have names ending with 'abad' such as Sikanderabad, Moradabad, Muzzafarabad, Hyderabad. A more significant phonetic resemblance exists between the English 'shire' which suffixes so many English areas, and the Urdu or Hindustani 'shehr', which means town or city and this term, also suffixes Indian settlements or towns. Thus a couple of the Princes at Princess Ujala's *swayamvara* are Princes of famous 'shehrs'.

Bharatian empire) has come to Maha Bharat to take part in a prestigious stage production. Princess, a Bharatian actress (who plays the leading role of Princess Ujala in the play) feels attracted by him. She is however wooed in turn by Chanakaya, another actor who plays an important part, that of Prince Chanakaya, opposite Socrates in the play and resents the attention being given to the foreigner. The play commences.

A *swayamvara* is being held for the hand of Princess Ujala. Only princes can participate in the ceremony and many young princes from all over Maha Bharat have come to participate in the ceremony. The presence of Socrates a prince from Blighty raises eyebrows. According to tradition the Princess makes a shortlist of candidates to then throw a challenge to the short listed candidates...

Last comment. While aspects of several fictional characters bear clear resemblance to historical personages in the British – Indian colonial context, the plays general theme is however of a much broader and more universal application and the play could be staged anywhere from Mongolia to Cameroon, without losing relevance.

The play got finished. The assignment continues

RT
Pristina
12.12.2002

Acknowledgements

In writing this play, I would like to acknowledge the help and encouragement given to me by various persons. In particular I would like to thank Diana Gashi, Nasir Peci, Yves del Monaco, Jeffrey, Violeta, Drita, Yuta, Hector, Francoise Simard, Emily Sanson, Kauru, Agim Bajrami, Mirvet, Michael, Luiz Alvarez, Aferdita, Sabria, Gerlinde and Vlora.

Dramatis Personale

Mrs. Bajaj	:	a rich widow
Poonam	:	her daughter, the bride
Ravinder	:	the bridegroom
Mrs. Arora	:	the bridegroom's mother
Papaji	:	Mr. Arora, the bridegroom's father
Gulshan	:	Poonam's *rakhi* brother, who runs an electronic shop in Ghaziabad.
Madhu	:	a supreme court lawyer, who is also Mrs. Bajaj's niece
Mr. Pujari	:	a matrimonial agent
Mr. Gupta	:	a rich businessman, with a slightly handicapped daughter

A judge, a public prosecutor, a lawyer, a police inspector and three constables.

Scene 1

(Inside a card room in a club, a Judge is sitting across the table with a Public Prosecutor. They are both in their late thirties and are waiting for their cards companion, a defence lawyer to arrive so that they can begin their game of rummy.)

Prosecutor: I don't think the gentleman is going to come. Shall we play a hand?

Judge: Let's wait awhile. It's not much fun if only two are playing.

Prosecutor: This is the second time this week that he hasn't turned up.

Judge: He had said he would be here sharp at six. Is he like this as far as Court appearances go as well then?

Prosecutor: No, Judge, he wouldn't dare - especially not in front of you. You had the reputation of being a tough judge in Banaras, I hear.

Judge: No, I don't think I'm very tough. It's true however that I don't tolerate unpunctuality in my Court.

Prosecutor: You would have dismissed his case in default of appearance then?

Judge: Yes, that'd teach him to be on time the next occasion.

Prosecutor: (smiling) Well, on this occasion we can't dismiss his case- since there is none - but perhaps we should impose some costs.

Judge: (laugh) Yes, perhaps we should. Get him to pay for the refreshment, you think?

Prosecutor: (laughing) Why not? !

Prosecutor: Should we order some coffee while we wait for Mr lawyer? Yes (shouts) waiter!

Enter Waiter

Waiter: Yes Sir.

Prosecutor: A pot of coffee please

Judge: (murmurs) Some sandwiches..

Prosecutor: And a plate of cheese sandwiches.

Exit Waiter

Prosecutor: So how do you like it here in Ghaziabad, Judge? How does it compare with Banaras?

Judge: It's all right. The accommodation is quite spacious. It's better than what I had in Banaras.

Prosecutor: And your wife? Does she like it?

Judge: She hasn't arrived here as yet. I thought I would reach first, settle down a bit, and then call her down.

Prosecutor: So, you are alone at home in the evenings, getting bored. I suppose you must watch a lot of television.

Judge: (grumbling). How much television can a person watch? And so many channels are just showing these song and dance routines from the cinema.

Prosecutor: That's true. (suggestively) There was recently a raid at a video parlour in Princes Market. These days I have in *my* possession some two hundred and fifty blue films seized during that raid.

Judge: (not taking the bait) I see. I suppose that the police have given them to you temporarily. It's case property, isn't it?

Prosecutor: (eagerly) That's right, Judge. If you like I can loan a few of the better ones to you.

Judge: (outraged) What on earth for? I couldn't bear to watch that disgusting stuff. (pauses) I suppose you need to watch them as part of your official duties as public prosecutor.

Prosecutor: (has understood the Judge's aversion) That's right, of course, Judge. I wouldn't dream of watching them otherwise. 1t was only in that context that I had suggested that you might like to view them.

Judge: (mollified somewhat) Oh, well, I understand. No, thanks, Mr Prosecutor. I won't have to deal with those obscenity and pornography cases. I will however be dealing with criminal matters which I am not completely familiar with. In Banaras, you see, I dealt mostly with civil cases. The District Judge here has told me that I will be asked to handle cases pertaining to crimes against women. Rape, wife battery and dowry related complaints.

Prosecutor: Section 498A, Indian Penal Code?

Judge: That's right. Did you read the papers today? There is a seminar being held at the India International Centre tomorrow by the Harassed Husbands Society on the misuse of Section 498 A. What do you make of it?

Prosecutor: It's a beneficial piece of legislation, Judge, dealing with the subject of cruelty to married women. It provides punishment of upto three years imprisonment for any husband (or his relative) who subjects his wife to cruelty. It's generally dowry related, but not necessarily so.

Judge: (impatiently) I know all that! What I'm asking you is whether you think there is some merit in the accusation that the police often falsely implicate an innocent husband and his parents at the behest of the woman's family?

Prosecutor: (shaking his head vigorously) Not true at all, Judge. The police are acting in compliance of the law. Take a typical case where the girl has returned to her parental home as a result of the harsh treatment of the in-laws, but the property which she did bring with her by way of dowry has not been returned. Now the girl's family makes a complaint to the police that is to the effect that the boy's family is not returning the dowry items. They provide the police with a list of all the items, ranging from sofa-sets, refrigerators, the girl's jewellery items, the works. The police conduct a surprise raid, seize all this property and give it back to the girl's family. Now what is wrong with that?

Judge: Nothing at all. However do the police need to verify the ownership of all these individual items before they go ahead with the raid?

Prosecutor: No.

Judge: Now that's the issue! Now the girl's family could simply concoct a list in order to harass the in-laws.

Prosecutor: Yes they could. What's the alternative? If they don't seize the property, the in-laws may in time dispose it off quietly, and then claim it was returned. The whole idea is that in this marriage game everybody must keep receipts, showing ownership. If the boy's. family have receipts they could show these to the police, and claim the seizures were illegal. The girl's family now-a-days have started keeping receipts, because there are no longer any guarantees that the marriage will last. After three years the girl may be back in her family house, having lost her virginity and the family fortune. Now, they have to dig up a dowry for her once again if there is to be any possibility of her remarriage, especially since she now since the stigma of being a divorcee.

Judge: That's true. Yet it's also because of the stigma of divorce, that the girl's family may develop a vengeful attitude and make false accusations. A boy and girl may part ways because they do not get along. They do not get along and the boy wants a divorce. The girl doesn't and since she and her family have to bear the social brunt of it, in a vengeful act, they put a false case on the boy's family alleging mistreatment and harassment on account of dowry.

Prosecutor: That's perfectly plausible, and I don't deny that it happens sometimes.

Judge: This whole thing has become a weapon in the hands of the girl's family. If the girl goes to the police and makes a statement that they tried to kill her, the police do not in such cases consider the prima facie plausibility of the allegations. They have their orders to go to the boy's house and immediately arrest all the implicated parties.

Prosecutor: On the other hand, judge, what if the allegations are true, which they very often are.

Judge: This doesn't mean that an innocent party should suffer. Our common law inherited from the British tells us that it is far better a hundred guilty persons go unpunished than one innocent person be falsely punished.

Prosecutor: That was meant in a different context, judge. I could perhaps accept that it is better that a hundred murderers go scot-free than an innocent person is falsely sentenced for having committed a murder. However this is not that case. Here, the innocent may suffer for being falsely accused, but the truth will soon out in the court.

Judge: But they will suffer. How they will suffer!

Prosecutor: Not so much really, judge. They have their remedies in civil law. They could seek damages for defamation

Judge: You know how slowly our Courts function. It will take years before the cases are decided and justice is done. But I do understand the issue better now. This is really, what do they call it, a catch 22 situation. Last year I had visited Europe briefly to attend a judge's convention. I found they are using only electricity for cooking purposes. It's all because we still use cooking gas and kerosene that these particular kinds of kitchen accidents take place.

Prosecutor: Cooking gas is perfectly safe, judge, unless the cylinder bursts. It's only kerosene stoves that can sometimes be a little tricky. Let me tell you, that in my experience ninety-five per cent of these so-called kitchen fires involving daughter-in-laws are engineered. They are set up by the in laws who try and make it look like an accident. The most important thing you need to consider in these cases is the forensic evidence.

Judge: How do you mean?

Prosecutor: To give you an example, there was this dowry death case which came to me six months ago where it was being claimed as usual by the in laws that the girl's *sari* had caught fire accidentally while she was cooking in the kitchen. We got our forensic experts to conduct a thorough examination of not only the kitchen but of also the other rooms in the house.

Judge: And what did they find out?

Prosecutor: They found that the walls of the couple's bedroom bore strong trace of carbon deposit. You see in this case the girl had actually been set on Fire in the bedroom, and it was only somewhat later, that her body was pushed towards the kitchen , to make it look like an accident. When a human body weighing fifty, sixty kilos starts burning, a lot of smoke is generated, and this will certainly have its impact on the walls of the room, even if she has been there only a few minutes, (turns triumphant) I managed to get all three convicted in that case mother-in-law, husband and father-in-law. The defence simply couldn't explain the lab findings concerning the bedroom walls.

Judge: (rubbing his chin) That's very interesting. As I was telling you, I have now been assigned to deal with these kinds of cases, so it's useful to have this kind of information

Prosecutor: Let me tell you about this girl Poonam's case, which is likely to come up in Court very soon.

Judge: Please go ahead.

Scene 2

(The scene takes place in a small office, with simple though adequate furnishings. On the walls are hung prints of various Gods and Goddesses. An incense stick is burning. Mr Pujari, the matrimonial agent is sitting opposite a black mahogany desk. Various files and folders have been arranged methodically and placed on the desk. Facing Mr Pujari and Mrs Arora, Papaji her husband, and their son Ravinder. The office appears to be part of a large house)

Mrs Arora: (addressing pujari)... and as we were telling you *bhai sahab,* we are on the lookout for a suitable girl for Ravinder *beta.*

Pujari: (looks at his watch) Oh, it's seven o'clock! *bahenji,* will you excuse me for two minutes. I have to just go in and quickly check my e-mail. There are some important non-resident Indian families who are also on the lookout for *a* suitable girl. I won't be long. I just want to see if their letters have arrived.

Mrs Arora: (grumpily) All right, but please don't take a long time.

Pujari: I won't be long at all.

Exit Pujari

Mrs Arora: This is all your fault, Papaji.

Papaji: My fault! What do you mean my dear?

Mrs Arora: You never even spoke to Guptaji once about his daughter Sumitra for our Ravinder, otherwise there would have been no need to meet this matrimonial agent, Mr Pujari and to have to pay his commission.

Papaji: But one of Sumitra's legs is shorter than the other.

Mrs Arora: (scornfully) How does that matter? Are you going to get her to play football? In any case, it's scarcely noticeable. Mr. Gupta is a multimillionair, and she is his only child. All our problems would have been solved.

Papaji: Listen, it wouldn't have worked out even had I spoken to Guptaji (shakes his head) he would have turned down the suggestion. No question about Sumitra and Ravinder. As you say Mr Gupta is such a rich businessman and Sumitra is his only daughter we are small fry for the likes of his family.

Mrs Arora: Humph.You never even tried. You coward!

Ravinder: Mummyji, please don't quarrel.

Re-enter Pujari

Pujari: (in a satisfied tone) Yes, there were eight e-mails in all. I will read them all later in the night. (sits down)

Mrs Arora: As we were telling you, *bhaisahab*, we also are on the lookout for a suitable girl for Ravinder.

Pujari: There is a lovely girl, *one* Sunita. Very beautiful.

Ravinder: (eagerly) Do tell us, Uncle.

Papaji: Is she a sober, decent girl Mr. Pujari? That's the main thing you know.

Pujari: Oh. Yes! She is a very dutiful girl. She will serve all of you unflinchingly.

Papaji: What do you say Ravinder?

Ravinder: Sounds good. Papaji.

Papaji: Well, then let's go and see her. She seems to be the right sort for you Ravinder. We don't want a fast girl, do we? The girls from Delhi can be very fast.

Mrs Arora: Wait a minute, both of you! Pujariji, what does the girl's father do?

Pujari: He retired from the Ministry as a Head Clerk I'm afraid he doesn't enjoy a very high status.

Mrs Arora: Oh, that doesn't matter. We know a lowly police official in Ghaziabad... (turns to Papaji). Do you remember him, dear, that Inspector Baljit? (turns back to pujari) This man has built a fabulous three-storey mansion in Ghaziabad. It would do a minister in the government proud.

Ravinder: It's so elegantly furnished from the inside as well, Mummy. It has marble flooring inside, do you remember?

Mrs Arora: That's right. As we were telling you Pujariji, the job itself doesn't matter. Even clerks in the Ministry can make pots of money. Why, the other day someone was telling me about a junior engineer in the Delhi Development Authority who drives around in an Opel Astra.

Pujari: I'm sorry to have to disappoint you, Madam. This girl's father was a very honest fellow. Never made an extra rupee on the side. They live in a rented L.I.G flat in Janakpuri.

Ravinder: But she is beautiful, according to you . . .

Pujari: That's right, son.

Papaji: And she has a heart of gold.

Pujari: That 's right , Papaji.

Mrs Arora: (addressing Ravinder and Papaji) Keep quiet, both of you!! What on earth are we going to do with a heart of goId? What we need is a purse of goId. A purse of gold! Let's not waste time in discussing this God-forsaken family. Really, Pujariji, you should know better then to suggest such a girl for Ravinder. Not suitable at all.

Papaji: (hesitatingly) May be dear, we should at least see this girl ...

Mrs Arora: Whatever for? Papaji, you are really the limit. Are you Ravinder's father or his enemy? These people don't even have their own house to live in. Moreover, even their rented accommodation is Lower Income Group.

Papaji: (wearily) All right, dear. You know best

Mrs Arora: We have come all the way from Ghaziabad to meet you, Pujariji. You have been highly recommended to us. Surely you won't disappoint us. Find us a suitable girl. We will pay you more than your usual commission if necessary.

Pujari: (thoughtfully) Well ... there **is** another girl . . . Poonam. Mrs Bajaj's daughter.

Ravinder: Is she beautiful, Uncle?

Pujari: Not as attractive as Sunita, but certainly well above average.

Mrs Arora: Let's not talk anymore about this Sunita, shall we? Who is this other girl, Pujariji? Poonam , her name is, you said ....

Pujari: She is Mrs Bajaj's daughter. The girl has just finished doing a course in fashion Designing form South Delhi Polytechnic. They live in Model Town, in a large bungalow built on a thousand square yard plot. It's their own house.

Mrs Arora: What does the girl's father do?

Pujari: Oh, Mrs Bajaj is a widow. Her husband, the late Mr Sohan Lal Bajaj was a well-known , successful businessman. He died over two years ago.

Mrs Arora: Does Poonam have any brothers and sisters?

Pujari: *Oh,* no. She is an only child, (pauses) Apart from the house they live in, they own a factory at Naraina and have another biggish plot in Faridabad.

Mrs Arora: This sounds like a good family, Pujariji.

Pujari: I know the family quite well. The girl is extremely good-hearted.

Papaji: Wonderful!

Ravinder: When can we see the girl. Uncle?

Pujari: Let's see. Wait a minute. I think I have some photographs of her. (He takes out an envelope kept inside a file folder and withdraws some photographs. He gives these to Ravinder, who takes a long look at them, then passes them around.)

Mrs Arora: Pujariji, we would like to meet this family. When can this be arranged?

Pujari: (scratching his head) I don't know. You see, there is a line of suitors for the girl.

Mrs Arora: (haughtily) There is no dearth of suitors for our Ravinder either.

Pujari: (in a placating tone) I know, I know. The girl's mother Mrs Bajaj had come to my place only last month. I have already arranged a meeting between her and a non-resident Indian family this coming Saturday. This NRI family is coming with their son, a Chartered Accountant working in London. My feeling is that the boy and girl may like each other and the marriage may get fixed this Saturday itself. Mrs Bajaj is keen to get her daughter married off soon.

Ravinder: Can't we go and see the girl one day earlier, say on Friday. Uncleji?

Pujari: That's a very intelligent suggestion. Ravinder *beta*. Let me check my diary, (flips through a diary kept on the desk) Nooooo... (his voice turns regretful) No. I'm sorry, son. I wish it was possible, but I'm simply too busy with my other engagements this entire week.

Mrs Arora: Pujariji, we have been taking so much of your valuable time. I think we should pay you at least double your usual charges.

Pujari: No, no. That's not necessary.

Mrs arora: No, we insist! (turns to Papaji) Papaji, make out a cheque for Rs. 5000 in favour of Pujariji now as advance payment.

Pujari: Oh, that's not really necessary, madam. It's actually not really possible for me to be free on Friday. I have prior commitments, which I cannot get out of. However, if on Saturday nothing works out between Poonam and this Chartered Accountant boy, I will let you know immediately and I can then arrange a meeting for you to see her.

Mrs Arora. Did I say double, Pujariji I'm feeling so ashamed of myself That's not what I meant at all. What I actually wanted to say was that if this marriage between Poonam and Ravinder gets arranged we will pay you five times your usual fees. It's such a fine family after all.

Pujari: (emphatically) There is no doubt about it. Mrs Bajaj is an extremely generous woman and her daughter Poonam is the apple of her eye. They are such simple people, in spite of being so rich. Their Model Town house itself must be worth twenty million and the Naraina factory must be worth another thirty million, at the very least.

Mrs Arora: Papaji, you haven't written out that cheque as yet, have you? Make it ten thousand.

Pujari: It's not necessary, madam. It's not necessary at all.

Mrs Arora: You cannot refuse pujariji. We won't leave this place until you agree.

Pujari: Oh, Madam, you make it so difficult to refuse.

(Papaji finishes writing out the cheque, which he then hands over to Pujari.)

Pujari: (accepting the cheque) All right then. I will somehow manage things such that I'm free on Friday evening.

Mrs Arora: That's simply great. It's fixed then.

Pujari: You leave me with no option. I have some really pressing engagements this entire week and if it had been anybody else I would have refused. But you are such a wonderful lady, Mrs Arora, it is not within my powers to refuse you.

Mrs Arora: (simpering) You flatter me, Pujariji.

Pujari: Let me give you the address (scribbles it on a piece of paper). We will meet on Friday evening at six o'clock at Model Town. Is that agreed? Okay. I will arrange it with Mrs Bajaj.

Scene 3

(The scene takes place inside Mrs Bajaj's house at Model Town. The set is divided into two sections. One section shows the drawing room of the house, where Mrs Bajaj, her niece Madhu, Gulshan and Mr Pujari, the matrimonial agents are all seated on sofas. The second, smaller half of the set represents a bedroom inside which Poonam, the would be bride is preening herself in front of the dressing table. There is a lit passage leading to the rear of the house from the drawing room. The time as seen from a wall-clock in the drawing room is five forty-five in the evening.)

Pujari: These are the boy's photographs (hands over some photographs to Mrs Bajaj)

Mrs Bajaj: (approvingly) Quite a good looking boy. Looks to be decent as well. Here. Madhu, what do you think?

Madhu: (takes a look) Looks are not important, Auntyji. He is certainly quite handsome, though. (She passes over the photographs to Gulshan)

Mrs Bajaj: Poonam insists that the boy should be smart and handsome. In a way she is quite right. After all you have to see the fellow's face across the pillow for the rest of your life-Gulshan, what do you think?

Gulshan: From the photograph, he seems to be all right.

Mrs Bajaj: Have you seen this boy before? He happens to be from your town.

Gulshan: As you very well know, Auntyji, I've been in Ghaziabad for only a year now.

Mrs Bajaj: Yes, of course. It already seems such a long time. Poonam and I miss you so much. It was so much nicer when you lived close by. Couldn't you have somehow continued to stay there

Gulshan: No, Auntyji. There is very little money in teaching martial arts. Now with this electronics shop that I've started, in six months, I'm already making three times as much as I did from the martial arts centre.

Mrs Bajaj: Oh, I sure you'll do even better in time to come, Gulshan *beta*-you're such a hard worker -but we really do miss having you close by Especially Poonam.

Madhu: She was a regular student of yours, wasn't she, Gulshan *bhaiya*?

Gulshan: The most regular student.

Madhu: What was it you taught her? Judo? Karate?

Gulshan: That's all outdated, Madhuji. Now-a-days the craze is to learn taekwondo. It involves a great deal of use of the legs.

Madhu: I should have also attended your classes, Gulshan.

Mrs Bajaj: Really, Madhu ? Isn't fighting in Court day in and day out good enough for you that you also want to learn this- this taekwondo.

Madhu: Oh, Auntyji, It would have been fun - and useful.

Mrs Bajaj: I don't know what is happening to the younger generation of girls now-a-days.

Madhu: (to Gulshan) Was Poonain a good learner?

Gulshan: The best!! I tell you, Madhuji , Auntyji. This girl could have become a martial arts expert in a very short period of time. She has an incredibly flexible body.

Madhu: And loads of energy!

Mrs Bajaj: That's why we are getting her married off.

Madhu: You shouldn't be in such a hurry, Auntyji. She's very young as yet.

Mrs Bajaj: It's best to marry while you're young. That's what Mr Bajaj used to say.

Gulshan: (looking closely at Ravinder's photographs) You know, Auntyji, in recent years, Ghaziabad has also spread out like Delhi. It is not possible to know everyone. However, if you wish, I can make enquiries about the boy and his family.

Mrs Bajaj: I don't think it is necessary in this case. Pujariji says he knows the family and they are decent people. That's good enough for me.

Pujari: Oh, *yes bahenji*· The boy is one in a million.

Gulshan: Is our Poonam any less? If he is one in a million then she is one in a billion. Where is Poonam, by the way?

Mrs Bajaj: She is in the next room changing. Madhu dear, just go and see why she is taking so long . Show her the photographs as well.

Exit Madhu

(She goes into the adjoining room. where Poonam is getting ready.)

Madhu: Poonam, what's the matter? What's taking you so long?

Poonam: My hair! It's taking me ages to straighten it out.

Madhu: Come, let me help you out.

(She starts brushing Poonam's hair vigorously. Meanwhile, in the other room Pujariji and Mrs Bajaj are talking.)

Pujari: They should be coming anytime now I had told them to come at six sharp.

Mrs Bajaj: There goes the bell ! It must be them. Gulshan dear, please open the door.

(Gulshan goes to open the door)

Enter Mrs Arora, Papaji and Ravinder

Mrs Arora: Namasteji . . .

Mrs Bajaj: Namasteji. . . Come in. Come in. please be seated.

(Papaji, Mrs Arora and ravinder all take their seats)

Mrs Bajaj: Did you have a problem in finding the house?

Ravinder: None at all, Auntyji.

Mrs Arora: Ravinder is very familiar with Delhi roads. Every week he drives down in his Maruti to make purchases from Chandni Chowk.

Mrs Bajaj: I see. pujariji was telling me that you have a shop in Ghaziabad.

Pujari: Oh, yes. They have a very large shop in Princes Park. It's the most prestigious shopping centre in Ghaziabad.

Mrs Arora: Something like Connaught Place in Delhi.

Mrs Bajaj: All of you have very long lives. Pujariji had just finished saying that you would be coming anytime, when the bell rang.

Papaji: What are we going to do with long lives, *bahenji*? All we want is that our children should be happy.

Mrs Bajaj: (understandingly) My late husband Bajaj *sahah* used to say the same thing.

Mrs Arora: (sympathetically) What happened to him?

Mrs Bajaj: A heart attack.

Mrs Arora: Oh, so unfortunate! These days everyone is suffering from heart ailments. Even Mr Arora was admitted to Batra Hospital last year following a heart attack. We didn't spare any money. We wanted the very best treatment for him.

Mrs Bajaj: (looking concerned) Oh, is that so?

Papaji: I always maintain, *bahenji,* that for people in our age group, life cannot be trusted anymore.

Mrs Arora: As a matter of fact, Ravinder wanted to delay getting married, but told him that *beta* it's high time you got married and settled down with a nice, decent girl.

Papaji: *Bahenji,* all we want is a nice, decent girl. Pujariji has been singing praises about your Poonam.

Mrs Arora: That's right, dear. All we are concerned with is the girl. Nothing else matters. If Ravinder and Poonam are happy, then we are happy.

Mrs Bajaj: (wipes a tear) That's what my late husband used to say as well. (turns to Ravinder) *Beta,* have some *burfi.* Don't feel shy. (turns to Gulshan) Gulshan, please offer...(Gulshan promptly offers sweets and dry fruits to Mr and Mrs Arora) This is Gulshan, Poonam's *rakhi* brother. He is like a family member for us. As a matter of fact, he too has a shop in Ghaziabad.

Papaji: Where is your shop, Gulshanji ?

Gulshan: Uncleji, I have a scooter and motor-cycle repair shop in *Kabadi bazaar*. Please do come sometime.

Mrs Arora: Of course we will, although we never go that side actually. It's a very smelly area, because of that big gutter nearly.

Gulshan: (swallowing his pride) That's true.

Mrs Arora: It will be better if you come to our shop in Princes market. There are all kinds of diseases one can catch in *Kabadi bazaar*.

Mrs Bajaj: (changing the topic) Ravinder *beta,* what kind of girl are you looking for?

Ravinder: Frankly, Auntyji. Pujariji has spoken so highly of your daughter and you yourself have so impressed me that I am willing to marry your daughter even without meeting her.

Mrs Bajaj: (visibly flattered) You flatterer! You must be having your preferences at least!

Ravinder: No, seriously Auntyji, after meeting you and seeing, your daughter's photograph's I am satisfied. The rest is upon you and my parents.

Papaji: He knows that whatever we decide, we have only his welfare at heart.

Mrs Arora: Such an obedient child.

Mrs Bajaj: Isn't he? In this day and age it is difficult to find children such as these.

Pujari: What did I tell you, bahenji? He is a very good boy.

Papaji: In our times this used to be very common. I never even got a chance to *see* Mrs Arora before our marriage. I was told that I didn't agree her father would shoot me off.

Ravinder: (laughing) Papaji, you always exaggerate.

Papaji: No, seriously, son, I am telling you the truth. In fact if it hadn't been for that threat.

Mrs Bajaj: 1t's difficult for today's generation to understand these things. These days children don't care a hoot for the wishes of their parents.

Ravinder: By the Way, Auntyji, how much rent do you pay for this house? A friend of mine is interested in taking up accommodation in these parts.

Mrs Bajaj: No. son this is not a rented accommodation.

Pujari: I think I forgot to tell you, Ravinder. This is their own house they are living in. (chuckles at the absurdity of any other possibility) No question of any rent to anyone!

Enter a maid, carrying a pot of tea with some more snacks in a Tray which she puts on the centre table, and withdraws

Mrs Bajaj: Let *me* make the tea. Ravinder *beta,* would you prefer a coke?

Ravinder: No, auntyji, tea is fine with me.

Mrs Bajaj: Don't be shy, son. At least have some of this *gajar ka halwa.*

Ravinder: (spoons some of the pudding on to his plate) Thanks, Auntyji.

Mrs Bajaj: This carrot pudding is home made. (proudly) Our Poonam has made it. It's her favourite pudding.

Papaji: In that case I will take some more. *(piles some more of the pudding on his plate)*

Mrs Arora: At least we have come to know something about dear Poonam's preferences.

Mrs Bajaj busies herself making tea and serving the visitors. Gulshan helps her. Meanwhile in the adjoining room, Madhu is talking to Poonam, whilst combing her hair

Poonam: What do you think, *didi?*

Madhu: What can I say, sweetheart? You have to form a judgement and make a decision. If you like, I can suggest that you and the boy talk privately in the other room.

Poonam: Don'I do that, *didi.* I feeI so shy.

Madhu: Poonam, this is a very important decision you have to take. I think you should at least talk to the boy before making up your mind.

Poonam: No, *didi,* please don't make any such suggestion. It's not necessary for us to talk unless he wants to.

Madhu: I'm sure he will want to.

Poonam: (fondling the photographs) Isn't he very handsome, *didi*?

Madhu: I daresay he is quite good looking - but these things are not so important, my dear.

Poonam: His eyes are so soft and his hair is so thick.

Madhu: I can hear voices. They have come. I think you should go in now.

Poonam: You go first , *didi*. I'II follow you in a while.

Madhu: All right then, but come soon. The boy's side don't like to be kept waiting.

Enter Madhu

Papaji: Come in, come in my dear. Don't feel shy.

Madhu: (politely) I think you are addressing the wrong person perhaps.

Mrs Arora: This man!! I tell you.

Ravinder: (laughing) Papaji. have you forgotten the girl's photographs already?

Mrs Bajaj: Never mind, never mind. These small mistakes do happen. Aroraji this is my niece, Madhu. She is an Advocate practising in the Supreme Court.

Papaji: Oh, I see. How clumsy of me!

Mrs Bajaj: She is my late brother's daughter. She has been practising in the Courts for many years now. (addresses Madhu) How many years has it been now, my deal?

Madhu: Fifteen years, Auntyji.

Mrs Bajaj: She is like my very own daughter. As dear to me as Poonam is.

Mrs Arora: (addressing Papaji) How could you ever make such a mistake? Can't you see that this is a mature woman? Our Poonam is only nineteen, isn't she?

Gulshan: She celebrated her nineteenth birthday only last month.

Poonam Enters Smiling Demurely

Mrs Arora: Come in, come in my dear. (wise-cracking) You have really made us wait.

Ravinder: But it was certainly worth the wait.

Mrs Bajaj: What a clever boy?! He knows just the right thing to say.

Papaji: Have some shame, boy. Don't you have any sense of propriety?

Mrs Bajaj: Well, I know that these days boys and girls like to talk to each other before deciding anything.

Madhu: I think that's a very good idea.

Mrs Bajaj: Ravinder *beta,* are you certain that you wouldn't like to do that? We can all go to the next -room, and leave you both alone here to talk for a while.

Ravinder: It's not. necessary for me, Auntyji. I can decide matters very fast. I have liked the girl. It now remains for her to decide. Of course we can sit here and talk if she would like that.

Papaji: *Behanji,* we are very open minded, liberal people.

Mrs Bajaj: Poonam...

Poonam covers her face with her hands and rushes out of the room

Mrs Bajaj: She is feeling too shy to say anything.

Gulshan: This means she is agreeable.

Mrs Bajaj: One can't be sure. Gulshan dear, will you go and ask her?

Gulshan goes to the next room, speaks to Poonam, who signals a tearful yes. He returns to living room

Gulshan: She is agreeable.

Mrs Arora: Well, the boy and the girl have decided. Now it's all up to you, *bahenji*. What *is* your decision?

Mrs Bajaj: We will let you know on the phone at the earliest, after we have compared both their horoscopes. But now that we are together, would you like to ask us anything? please don't hesitate.

Papaji: *Bahenji,* we have liked your Poonam. We want only her. We are not concerned about any other matter. We don't trust astrology.

Mrs Arora: Papaji is perfectly right in what he says. We want a daughter for the house, not a daughter- in- law. I have always wanted a daughter. But *bahenji,* you also feel free to ask us anything you like.

Mrs Bajaj: Oh, no, nothing at all.

Mrs Arora: As far as we are concerned, we have told you that we are willing. We will wait for your decision. Now we will take your leave.

Exeunt Mrs Arora, Papaji and Ravinder

Mrs Bajaj: What did you think of them, Gulshan?

Gulshan: (reluctantly) They seem to be good people.

Mrs Bajaj: That's what I think. Very straightforward and decent people like us (laughs), Madhu, what do you think, my dear? Isn't it an excellent family?

Madhu: (slowly) I am not so sure. I think we should make a thorough enquiry, before proceeding any further.

Mrs Bajaj: Oh, you are being unnecessarily suspicious. It is. It's your training as a lawyer that makes you like that, I suppose. Pujariji knows the family very well, and he has recommended them. They didn't make any enquiries about our property or assets. Nothing imagine, that boy Ravinder even thought that this house was on rent.

Pujari: My job was to introduce both of you. I have done my job. The rest is upon you to decide. But, if you take my advice, don't lose this boy. He is a real gem.

Mrs Bajaj: And Poonam likes him too. I think I'll call them up in the morning and say yes.

Madhu: Don't be in such a hurry, Aunty.

Pujari: Mrs Bajaj is right, *beta.* You people should decide soon. The star is setting in fifteen days time. Astrologically speaking, the wedding should take place before that period or else you would have to wait another three months.

Madhu: Well, what's the hurry? Let's wait.

Mrs Bajaj: No. My late husband used to say. "I'll marry Poonam off as soon as she crosses eighteen." She turned nineteen last month. I want a quick marriage for her now.

Madhu: Pujariji, what about that NRI boy who was to come to see Poonam?

Pujari: They are to come tomorrow evening- but that's not a problem. I can easily cancel the appointment, if all of you agree to this match. However, do let-me know what you decide before eleven in the morning

Mrs Bajaj: You go ahead and cancel it, Pujariji. I don't want to send our Poonam off to a far off country. In Ghaziabad, at least she will be nearby... and dear Gulshan is also there.

Madhu: Aunty, you are hurrying things too much.

Mrs Bajaj: Don't worry, my darling. Are you Poonam's mother or am I? I the one who should be worried, not you. Anyhow, both you and Gulshan are staying over the night, aren't you? We will talk more in the night.

Pujari: I'll take your leave, madam.

Mrs Bajaj: Thank you, Pujariji. You have been a great help.

Exit Pujari

Mrs Bajaj: Now let's hear what the would be bride has to say. Go call Poonam, Gulshan.

Gulshan: Oh, she'll be in the next room. (shouts) Poonam!Poonam!!

Poonam: (from the adjoining room) Yes, *bhaiya,* what is it?

Gulshan: Come here, we want your opinion on something.

Poonam: *Bhaiya,* you come here. I'm changing !! I also want your opinion on something.

Gulshan: (standing up) Okay, let me go and check out the bride.

Madhu: Auntyji, you should have told them that this is not your house.

Mrs Bajaj: Don't be so naive, my dear. Nobody tells these things on their own. What do you say, Gulshan?

Gulshan: Well, they asked if it was rented accommodation and you said no, it wasn't. You didn't: say anything false. It was Pujariji who said you were the owner.

Mrs Bajaj: (triumphantly) Exactly!!

Gulshan: (still standing) I'll go and see what Poonam wants.

Mrs bajaj: Yes, go and talk to her. On such occasions, sisters need to talk to their brothers.

Gulshan exits to the next room

Poonam: Come, *bhaiya.* Have a seat.

Gulshan: What did you want to talk about?

Poonam: Oh, nothing in particular! Give me a minute, will you? Let me take off this heavy sari, and get into something more comfy. And will you shut that door please.

(Poonam then proceeds to take off the heavy sari she is wearing and humming a tune proceeds to undress to her undergarments. She is completely unconcerned at Gulshan's presence, though Gulshan , who is sitting silently, watching her undress is a bit conscious and uneasy. Meanwhile in the next room Madhu and Mrs bajaj are talking).

Mrs Bajaj: Would you like a glass of brandy, Madhu?

Madhu: Well, I don't mind. Are you having some?

Mrs Bajaj: I need a glass to cool down my nerves. All this excitement !! Wait here. I'll go and get it. I keep it locked in the cupboard, so that the servant's don't start getting any ideas. Once in a while, even when Mr Bajaj was there, I would have a glass, good for the blood pressure.

Madhu: Auntyji, you don't have to provide me with any justifications. This is not the first time we are having a drink.

Mrs Bajaj: Okay, I'll just be back. Here, read this *filmfare* in the meanwhile.

Exit Mrs Bajaj

(Madhu starts rifling through the pages of the magazine. In the next room. poonam has changed into a pyjama suit)

Poonam: Now tell me, *bhaiya*.

Gulshan: What can I say? you're the one getting married.

Poonam: Not until you say so.

Gulshan: Well...I don' t know what to say.

Poonam: If you don't like him. bhaiya, I won't marry him. This is important for me, so tell me what you think frankly.

Gulshan: Well, really, they seem fine.

Poonam: They don't seem fine. I didn't like the way the boy's mother spoke about *Kabadi bazaar*.

Gulshan: (embarrassed) look, people talk this way. One can not do anything. But the boy seemed okay.

Poonam: Yes, he did didn't he? That's what matters really. All right, if you say so, but on one condition.

Gulshan: Yes?

Poonam: You have to come to see me at my in-laws house in Ghaziabad as frequently as you came to this house when you lived close by.

Gulshan: All right I agree (a bit sadly). So, it's wedding bells for you my dear sister.

Poonam: (hugs him) Don't tease me, *bhaiya*.

Gulshan: (strokes her face) My darling sister!

Poonam: (suddenly) I know what, *bhaiya*. let go upstairs to the terrace.

Gulshan: Upstairs? At this time?

Poonam: Yes. why not! There's a full moon tonight. I've spread out a *chatai*. it'll be nice and cool.

Gulshan: (hesitantly) Well ..okay.

Poonam: And you can also help me practice some kick movements, let me take advantage of your presence here today.

Exeunt Poonam and Gulshan

Enter Mrs Bajaj

(Mrs Bajaj comes in carrying a tray with a bottle of brandy, and some snacks. She places this on the table and sits down on the sofa.)

Mrs Bajaj: *Uf,* I am exhausted. Madhu, now you make the drinks.

Madhu: (smiling) Okay. With coke and ice?

Mrs Bajaj: Yes, of course. Somebody might drop by suddenly. And hide the bottle, behind the sofa or somewhere.

(Madhu starts mixing the drinks)

Madhu: Patiala or small?

Mrs Bajaj: (laughs) Patiala for me, my dear.

Madhu: I'll have a small one to begin with. Tell you what. This bottle's almost finished. I'll pour the rest of it into a clean teapot, and keep a chilled *coke* bottle besides. That way we can keep refuelling.

Mrs Bajaj: (laughing) You and your ideas!! Is this how you drink in your office?

Madhu: Auntyji, I don't drink in chambers. And when I'm at home, I don't bother to hide the fact that I'm drinking. This is all for your benefit.

Mrs Bajaj: Well, for you it's okay, I suppose. You're a young girl. We older women have to be more careful. Especially... you know Mr Bajaj's family.

(Madhu finishes her self appointed tasks, and sinks back into the sofa)

Mrs Bajaj: (takes a sip) Oh. this is good!

Madhu: (sipping her drink) I still think you should have made it clear that you don't really own this house anymore.

Mrs Bajaj: Oh, you're too finicky, Madhu. It's not our responsibility to disclose these details. If they really want to know they should go to the land registry.

Madhu: You mean check the records even before they come here.

Mrs Bajaj: Before or after. Its their business to find out, not ours to tell them.

Madhu: You're not being practical, Auntyji.

Mrs Bajaj: I'm being very practical, my dear. This is the way things are done. After all, Mr Bajaj did buy the land and build the house. It was only in his last years that the business ran up big losses, and *Vadey Brahji* - his elder brother had to bail him out.

Madhu: And now the property is in his elder brother's name.

Mrs Bajaj: True, but under the family settlement, we can stay here for as long as we live. I tell you, Madhu, we are not obliged to disclose these internal family matters to any family who comes to our house looking for a bride for their son.

Madhu: Well, may be, there is something in what you say, Auntyji. My point is that these days' people are so greedy for dowry, one cannot be too careful. If they think that you are the owner of this house, they might not expect so much by way of dowry on the assumption that Poonam will eventually inherit this house, but once they find out that you are not the owner, which they eventually will, then they might be very disappointed. They might accuse the girl that not only has her family cheated them out of a good dowry; there's not even any property that she will inherit.

Mrs Bajaj: My God, Madhu, I didn't realise you were so calculating. Really!! What are you lawyers made of? What do you eat, may I ask? And what makes you think I won't give any dowry?

Madhu: I mean a good dowry.

Mrs Bajaj: Yes! A good dowry.

Madhu: You have the money, Auntyji?

Mrs Bajaj: Of course I have, my dear. Mr Bajaj opened a fixed deposit in Poonam's name six months after she was born, which was to mature upon her eighteenth birthday. Tax savings, you know, but also this is the situation. Parents have to start preparing for a girl's dowry, soon after she is born.

Madhu: Oh, I wish these stupid customs were not there. Do you know Auntyji, under the law it is no longer legally permissible to take or give dowry.

Mrs Bajaj: Nothing wrong with dowry!My father gave Mr Bajaj a handsome dowry when I got married. He couldn't have set up his business without the money. That's where the initial capital came from.

Madhu: Does this make it a good thing, Auntyji? People who have made these laws have devoted time and thought to it

Mrs Bajaj: These are our customs. You cannot simply make a law doing away with age-old customs and traditions. Dowry has always existed in our society, and will continue to remain. Madhu, look at it this way The boys inherit all the property, don't they? Now, it's only fair if the girl too is compensated in some way.

Madhu: Yes, but under the law the girl too is entitled to an equal share in the property.

Mrs Bajaj: What do these laws matter? I inherited a lot of property under the law-you know that but I gave it all away to my brothers.

Madhu: You made me file No Objection Certificates in the Succession Judge's Court last year, didn't you, despite my advice to the contrary.

Mrs Bajaj: (wearily) That's the way my father God bless his soul- would have wanted it to be. After all, he gave me a good dowry, didn't he?

Madhu: Do you know what the Succession Judge said to me, when I went to file the papers?

Mrs Bajaj: No, what?

Madhu: He said Indian women are like angels, writing away all their property rights in favour of their brothers. I only hope the dowry you have saved up for Poonam will be good enough for this family.

Mrs Bajaj: It will, it will. Don't worry. It's quite a tidy sum. And these people don't seem to be too greedy. Come now, you have tired me out with your arguments. Let's go and down. Now, where have this brother and sister disappeared? Never mind! This girl must be practising her taekwondo, if I know her. Come, let's go to the bedroom and continue our chat.

Scene 4

(Three weeks later, Poonam and Ravinder's wedding is celebrated with traditional pomp and splendour. The day after the wedding, the newlyweds, Gulshan, Papaji, Mrs Arora and Mrs Bajaj are all gathered at the latter's house.)

Papaji: As I was saying , madam, the arrangements were superb. The food was delicious. I could see the guests smacking their lips. Many of our relatives paid compliments.

Mrs Bajaj: I am so glad to hear that. All the credit for this goes to dear Gulshan. He has been working day and night making all the preparations for the wedding. I simply couldn't have managed on my own. All the arrangements had to be made at such short notice because of the setting star. (turns to Gulshan) I hope yours business hasn't suffered too much on account of all this work.

Gulshan: What are you saying, Auntyji? Is my business more importance to me than Poonam's wedding?

Mrs Bajaj: All right, all right. I am sorry if I have offended you. After all if we do not ask you to help, whom else will we ask? You are like a member of the family.

Mrs Arora: Do visit us sometime in Ghaziabad, Gulshan.

Gulshan: Oh, yes Auntyji, I will do that. In any case I will drop by Ravinder *bhaisahab's* shop, whenever I happen to go to Princes market.

Mrs Arora: Oh, but you may not find him there anymore.

Mrs Bajaj: Why, are you planning to dispose off the shop?

Mrs Arora: No, no, *bahenji*. Papaji alone can actually manage the chemist's shop. Ravinder *beta* wants to set up a shop by himself. Isn't that right, son?

Ravinder: That's right, mother.

Gulshan: Ravinder *bhai sahab*, shall I try and find out if a shop is available in *kabadi Bazaar*.

Mrs Arora: Certainly not! We don't want a shop there, amongst thieves and scoundrels. Ravinder will purchase another shop in Princes market itself.

Ravinder: That's right, mother. (he puts his arms around Poonam.) Now that I am married, I need a good set-up of my own.

Mrs Bajaj: I am so pleased to hear your plans, Ravinder. What business are you intending to carry out from the shop?

Ravinder: I want to open a retail outlet for selling surgical equipment, Auntyji. There is much more profit in that as compared to a chemists shop. On the opening day, you must come inaugurate the shop.

Mrs Bajaj: Thank you, *beta*. I will certainly come if you wish it. Now don't call me Auntyji any more. It sounds terribly formal. From today onwards I am also your mother and you will call me Mummyji.

Ravinder: (sounding pious) Very good, Mummyji.

(Everybody laughs)

Mrs Arora: The problem of course is that the price of shops in the Princes market area is very high these days.

Papaji: We will manage somehow.

Mrs Arora: It will be difficult, dear. Even if we buy him the shop- and it's two million rupees, not a small amount - he will still need five hundred thousand rupees to do up the shop and buy some of the initial equipment. It's well beyond our means.

Papaji: That's true, my dear.

Mrs Bajaj: (hesitantly) Perhaps I can help somewhat ....

Ravinder: Thank you, Mummyji. You truly care a lot for Poonam and me.

Mrs Arora: No. no. *bahenji.* We don't want to take any money from you. Papaji will try and take a loan from some persons in the market.

Mrs Bajaj: (says again) To the extent possible. I will try and help.

Mrs Arora: Well . . . If you insist.

Ravinder: Thank you, Mummyji. You are such a dear.

Mrs Bajaj: Not at all. After all whatever I have is meant only for you and Poonam. That reminds me, I have purchased your air tickets to Kathmandu. You want to leave tomorrow night, don't you?

Ravinder: That's correct, Mummyji.

Mrs Bajaj: (fiddles about in her handbag) Here. These are the tickets, (hands them over to Ravinder) Gulshan has already done the hotel reservations.

Gulshan: You are booked into the Oberoi Soaltee, the best hotel in Kathmandu

Ravinder: Thank you, Mummyji. I love you.

Mrs Bajaj: Not at all, son. I hope the two of you have a wonderful honeymoon. (takes out a bulky envelope from her handbag) And here is some pocket money for both of you, to spend in Kathmandu, (hands over packet containing cash to Ravinder).

Ravinder: It's not really necessary, Mummyji.

Mrs Bajaj: No, I insist.

Papaji: Keep it *beta.* Always listen to your elders.

Mrs Arora: Poonam is very quiet today. Are you all right, my dear?

Poonam: Oh yes, Aunty. It's just that I'm very tired. I didn't sleep a wink last night.

Papaji: (pinches his son's arm playfully) Naughty boy, Ravinder.

Mrs Arora: Poonam, you too must address me as Mummyji from now onwards. Is that understood?

Poonam: Of course, Mummyji.

Scene 5

(The house of Mr and Mrs Arora at Ghaziabad. There is a drawing room, and an adjoining bedroom. There is however additionally a well-exposed kitchen next to the drawing room. There is also a small, well-lit passage leading from the drawing room into what is possibly a second bedroom. Entrance to the stage can be both from the main entrance to the house, which leads to the drawing room, or from the passage. The drawing room in the Arora house doubles up as a drawing cum dining room, so in addition to the usual sofa set and decorative items, there is a dining table with six chairs. In the drawing room there hangs a large wall clock whose arms are operated from behind to show the passage of time.

A week earlier, Poonam and Ravinder have returned from their honeymoon at Kathmandu. It is eleven o'clock in the morning and Poonam is serving *aloo ka paranthas* to Ravinder for breakfast).

Ravinder: These *parantthas* are truly delicious. Shall I have another one?

Poonam: (pleased) If you like, darling.

Mrs Arora: (entering the dining room, a duster in her hand) Ravinder *beta,* are not you going to the shop?

Ravinder: In five minutes, mother.

Poonam: I'll just make another one for you in a jiffy.

Mrs Arora: How many have you eaten, Ravinder?

Ravinder: (hesitantly) Two.

Mrs Arora: That is enough then. Poonam, do not make any more *paranthas.* Ravinder always has only two in the morning.

Poonam: All right, Mummyji.

Ravinder: I wanted to eat another one, mother.

Mrs Arora: (somewhat disconcerted) Oh, I see. Well, in that case, Poonam . . .

(Poonam goes off into the kitchen)

Mrs Arora: Have you spoken to her about the money?

Ravinder: I have. She spoke to her mother on the phone yesterday. She will be sending a draft for two hundred thousand through Gulshan's hand tomorrow morning.

Mrs Arora: (shocked) What?! Only two hundred thousand !!

Ravinder: (in a pacifying tone) I told Poonam it wasn't much of a contribution. The shop itself will cost us at least two million and the equipment will be extra . According to her her mother says she doesn't have any money.

Mrs Arora: What the hell does she mean by saying that she doesn't have any more money? Didn't Pujariji mention a large plot in Faridabad ? Why can't they sell that off ?

Ravinder: The Haryana Urban Development Authority apparently acquired it for road widening purposes, and they were given compensation.

Mrs Arora: And the money ?

Ravinder: They spent it all on her wedding.

Mrs Arora: Humph. It couldn't have been a very big plot in that case. (thinks) They have the factory, don't they? Why can' t she sell off that factory at Naraina? Mr Pujari had told us that it was worth at least twenty million. With that kind of money in her hands she can easily cough up two, three million. We are only asking for one million.

Ravinder: I know, mother, but for some reason her mother doesn't want to sell off the factory.

Mrs Arora: Then let her put it in your name. At least that way . . .

Ravinder: Keep quiet, mother. She's coming.

Mrs Arora: (muttering) So what if she is coming ? I am not going to keep quiet over this.

(Poonam enters carrying a *parantha* on a plate)

Poonam: (putting it on Ravinder's plate) I haven't put any butter on top of this one. Okay?

Ravinder: Yes, thank you , Poonam makes terrific *paranthas,* mother.

Mrs Arora: Humph. That's all she is *good* for.

(Mrs Arora stalks out of the room)

Poonam: Why is Mummyji so annoyed with me? What. Have I done?

Ravinder: Don't look so concerned, darling. She is very moody sometimes. Just ignore her. She will be all right soon. Now just give me a peck on the cheek before I leave for office.

Poonam: Mummyji may see.

Ravinder: No, she's gone inside.

(Poonam gives him a peck on the cheek. Ravinder grabs her. They kiss for long. Just then Mrs Arora re-enters the room. She watches them angrily.)

Mrs Arora: (loudly) Humph. She is good at this as well.

(She leaves the room again. Poonam and Ravinder break apart.)

Poonam: I was telling you...

Ravinder: Don't worry, sweetheart. Mother's very moody today. She will be all right soon. Just wait for a couple of hours. You'll see. Now I'd better rush to the shop.

Poonam: All, right dear.

Exit Ravinder

(Poonam starts clearing the breakfast table. She lakes a mop and starts wiping the dining table. Just then Mrs Arora enters.)

Mrs Arora: Oh, my legs. My poor legs! They are aching so horribly.

Poonam: Mummyji, do you want me to press your legs?

Mrs Arora: Well, yes, you could do that.

(Mrs Arora lies down on a sofa. Poonam starts pressing her leg.)

Mrs Arora: (after a while) That's enough. Now go and dust the furniture. That table... (starts directing) Now these chairs. This table fan here. That's enough. Now go and make a cup of tea for me. I haven't had a decent cup of tea since the morning.

(Poonam goes into the kitchen to make some tea. Mrs Arora gets up from the sofa and commences an inspection of the cleaning. She picks up some dust from a small table.)

Mrs Arora: (addressing the audience) Doesn't even know how to dust properly!!

(She goes back to lie down on the sofa. Poonam returns carrying a set of tea on a tray. She sits down *next* to her mother-in-law and starts making the tea.)

Mrs Arora: Did you speak to your mother about the shop which Ravinder is planning to purchase?

Poonam: Yes, Mummyji.

Mrs Arora: What does she say?

Poonam: She says she will send the money through Gulshan *bhaiya*..

Mrs Arora: How much is she sending?

Poonam: I don't know.

Mrs Arora: What do you mean, you don't know? Don't you know how important this is? You should have asked.

Poonam: I think it is two hundred thousand rupees.

Mrs Arora: (scornfully) Two hundred thousand ! Hah! Do they think they have married their daughter to a sweeper? I tell you, people can be so shameless these days.

Poonam: Mummyji , she said she will try to arrange for some more money.

Mrs Arora: (mollified somewhat) She had better do that . Listen to me, Poonam. I think your mother doesn't realise how much this shop means to Ravinder. Why don't you, as her daughter explain this to her? See , it doesn't look nice for us to say anything. The shop is going to cost two million. She should, at the very least, contribute one million. Understand.

Poonam: Yes, Mummyji.

Mrs Arora: Talk to her today itself, in the evening, when Ravinder gets back from the shop. Understand.

Poonam: Yes, Mummyji.

Mrs Arora: After all, once Ravinder sets up this new shop and starts earning more money, you are going to be benefited as well. Am I saying something wrong?

Poonam: No, Mummyji.

Mrs Arora: At this rate, after marriage, instead of increasing his earnings, he is going to make less money. Why is he going to the shop so late these days?

Poonam: He just refuses to get up in the morning.

Mrs Arora: I can't believe that this is the reason. He used to get up perfectly well earlier.

Poonam: I will try my best to wake him up tomorrow and see that he goes with Papaji in the morning.

Mrs Arora: Do that ! After all if he is not there to manage things, business will suffer. Your Papaji actually has no head for business.

Poonam: Yes , Mummyji.

Mrs Arora: (Peremptorily) Now press my head. I have got a headache after having to explain all this to you.

(Poonam starts pressing Mrs Arora's head.)

Enter Papaji

Papaji: What is this I see? Heads are being pressed by daughters of the house.

Mrs Arora: (snapping) Mind your own business, if you don't want your head pressed, I'm not objecting , am I?

Papaji: In our days, Poonam *beta,* we never made the new daughter-in-law of the house do any household chores for one full month. My mother didn't let your mother-in-law lift a finger for one full month after our marriage. That is the tradition.

Mrs Arora: Humph. When I started doing household chores after a month, I was really made to slog, preparing lunch and dinner for a thirty-member household. A hundred *chapattis* to lunch and a hundred for dinner, apart from all the dishes. Today's girls don't have it in them to do any work. They make *two paranthas* for breakfast and think that they have done wonders . All they know is how to lie in bed and move their legs.

Papaji: Come, dear, is this the way to talk?

Mrs Arora: (furious) Are you going to teach me how to talk now? And why have you returned from the shop?

Papaji: I had this awful stomach ache, so I decided to *come* home and rest.

Mrs Arora: You and your stomach aches! Always making such a fuss. The son goes late to the shop and the father comes back after two hours. At this rate we will have to start borrowing provisions from the neighbours! To top it all, even the bride hasn't brought anything with her. If you ask me, she doesn't even deserve to sit on this sofa.

Papaji: What's wrong with you today? She is such an innocent girl and you are torturing her in this fashion.

Mrs Arora: Oh, so now she has turned you against me as well. I should have known. You men are all the same. No sense of loyalty. I hope Ravinder doesn't turn out like you.

Papaji: What's wrong with Ravinder ? He is a fine boy.

Mrs Arora: Now-a-days, once he gets into the bedroom with her, he just doesn't come out. I don't know where she has learnt all her tricks.

Papaji: (loudly now) Come now, behave yourself woman.

Mrs Arora: All right, all right. I am going to the bedroom. You can have a cosy chat with your precious daughter-in- law. Ooh, my legs are aching so. Nobody thinks of me . . .

Exit Mrs Arora

(After Mrs Arora has disappeared into an inner bedroom out of view of the audience, Poonam breaks down and starts weeping.)

Papaji: (putting his arm around her) Why are you crying?

Poonam: Nothing, Papaji.

Papaji: Tell me. *beta.* I'm like your father. Is it because of your mother-in-law's comments?

Poonam: No, Papaji.

Papaji: You will have to bear with her. She's like that. Look at me. I have borne with her all these years.

Poonam: (covering up for her mother-in-law) No, Papaji, it's not because of her. Ravinder was telling me that she is very moody.

Papaji: What is it, then? I think perhaps you are getting depressed staying in the house all the time. Why, you poor dear, you haven't even gone out since you returned from your honeymoon. Why don't you and Ravinder go out to the cinema tomorrow? I'll handle the shop by myself. It's no problem. Do you want me to talk to Ravinder?

Poonam: (sniffing) No, Papaji. I'll talk to Ravinder myself. I think you are right. It's staying at home all the lime that's been depressing me.

Papaji: Well, then, cheer up now. Give us a smile.

(Poonam smiles tremulously)

Papaji: And listen to me *beti*. If you have any problem , I repeat, any problem, you come straight and tell me . Do you understand?

Poonam: Yes, Papaji.

Papaji: I'll go and talk to your mother in law and tell her she mustn't treat you so badly.

Poonam: Thank you, Papaji . Thank you for everything.

(The stage darkens.The clock's needles move to show that it is now nine in the evening. There is a chiming sound. Poonam is sitting up in bed waiting for Ravinder.)

Enter Ravinder

Ravinder: Hullo, hullo. Is anyone at home? (He walks across the drawing room and enters the bedroom) So there you are!! Why is the house so quiet? Where is Papaji and Mummy?

Poonam: They've retired to their room. Do you know what time it is?

Ravinder: (airily) What time is it ? (looks at his watch) Nine o'clock. That's not so late. The day is still young.

Poonam: It may be young for you, but it's been very long for now.

Ravinder: I forgot to tell you. I had to take my friends out to dinner. They've been asking me for a treat ever since we came back from Kathmandu.

Poonam: (bitterly) 1 hope you enjoyed yourself!

Ravinder: Of course I did. (notices something is wrong) Hey, what's the matter? Are you all right? Has Mummy said something to you?

Poonam: What hasn't she said ?!

Ravinder: Listen to me. If you want to be happy in this house you have to listen to what mother says from one ear and take it out the other ear. Understand.

Poonam: I don't understand. Why does she have to be so mean?

Ravinder: Calm down, calm down. I'll talk to her. You know, if I can just lay my hands on this shop, the money will just roll in. We can then even take up a separate residence somewhere nearby. Would you like that, my dear?

Poonam: Yes, I would like that.

Ravinder: At the moment , we need one hundred thousand rupees very urgently, so that the shop doesn't slip out of our hands. You must explain to your mother just how important this shop is for us. Will you do that, love?

Poonam: (in a tearful tone, the day's events having finally taken their toll) Yes, of course.

Ravinder: (sympathetically) Oh, my poor dear. Looks like mother has been really nasty to you. Don't worry, once we have this shop in our hands, she'll be as sweet as sugar. I'll talk to her tomorrow. Tell her to behave. All right?

Poonam: (sniffing) All right.

Ravinder: Once the new business is up and running, we can move out and live separately. All right, my darling.

Poonam: (still sniffing) Yes.

Ravinder: Now come closer.

(He kisses her)

Ravinder: Now take that frown off your pretty face, and give me a smile.

(Poonam smiles hesitantly)

Ravinder: Will you do me a favour , Dearest?

Poonam: Yes, of course.

Ravinder: Will you wear your wedding dress?

Poonam: You mean right now?

Ravinder: Yes, of course.

Poonam: If someone were to come in...

Ravinder: Nobody will come. Papaji and Mummyji are both fast asleep. Who else can come?

Poonam: (hesitates) Well , all right.

(She gets up from the *bed,* searches out the dress from the wardrobe, and slowly puts it on.)

Ravinder: (is lying on the bed, watching) Now put on the jewellery as well.

Poonam: (startled) The jewellery too! Why?

Ravinder: So I can imagine it is actually that first night.

Poonam: You are mad!!

Ravinder: It's you who make me mad.

Poonam: Why do you want me to put on my jewellery?

Ravinder: Don't ask so many questions. Just do it.

(Poonam opens a locker inside the cupboard, from which she takes out a velvet case, and withdraws a *mangalsutra,* some earrings and some bracelets. She puts them on carefully, looking at herself in thc mirror. After she has finished, she goes and sits on the other side of the double bed.)

Ravinder: (evidently feasting his eyes) Now you look something.

Poonam: (coyly) You are just saying that.

(Ravinder attempts to kiss her.)

Poonam: Come on ji. Don't do anything. The *sari* will gel all crumpled up.

Ravinder: All right. Then take it off.

Poonam: Very funny! First, you ask. me to put it on, and then you ask me to take it off.

Ravinder: (fingers the mangalsutra on her neck) This looks quite expensive. It could fetch us quite a packet.

Poonam: (her mood immediately turns sour) Like this, you will sell me off too one day.

Ravinder: (placating her) Come on, my darling. Relax. Don't get so agitated.

Poonam: (angrily) These things cannot be sold, don't you know?

Ravinder: All right, all right. Forget I even mentioned it. Come now give me a kiss.

(A mollified Poonam kisses Ravinder.)

Ravinder: Last night was terrific, wasn't it?

Poonam: (shyly) And tonight. Isn't it going to be terrific tonight as well?

Ravinder: So you are in the mood.

Poonam: (shyly) Well, if we start early, we can finish early, otherwise you will get up late for breakfast tomorrow morning and Mummyji will once again be upset with *me*.

Ravinder: (doubtfully) I'm not so sure of that. Last night it was you only who kept on saying 'do it some more'.

Poonam: (a trace of indignation in her tone) Well, you finished off so quickly the first time.

Ravinder: (shocked) What?! What?!

Poonam: (gently) I mean to say, you know we women take longer ...

Ravinder: Take longer for what?

Poonam: Take longer to get satisfied.

Ravinder: Oh, well . . . (thinks for a minute) Tell me something, did you like the first position better, or the second.

Poonam: The second position, I think . but I've thought of an even better position for tonight.

Ravinder: (amazed) Really!! How? (to the audience) I know only two positions.

(Poonam explains to him what appears to be a fairly complicated position.)

Ravinder: (scratching his head) But how on earth will you remain in that position?

Poonam: (confidently) Don't worry I will manage.

Ravinder: Poonam, how do you know all this?

Poonam: (tearful) Are you doubting me?

Ravinder: (hastily) No, no. (pauses) It's just that you have the most incredible body.

Poonam: I bet you've said that to all your girl friends. You're the one who's had so many relations with women.

Ravinder: I don't mean that you have a wonderful figure. That of course you do have. The thing is that your body is so amazingly responsive . . . and so flexible. It's like rubber.

Poonam: That's what Gulshan used to say as well.

Ravinder: Gulshan?!

Poonam: My brother Gulshan, silly. He used to teach me martial arts.

Ravinder: Oh, oh, I see.

Poonam: Now don't delay any more - otherwise Mummyji will pull your ears tomorrow morning.

(Ravinder gives her a passionate kiss.)

Poonam: (breaking away) First go and pull the curtain.

Scene 6

(It is morning, and at the house of the Arora's in Ghaziabad, Poonam is serving breakfast. Mrs. Arora is also sitting on the breakfast table. The wall clock shows the time to be seven o'clock.)

Ravinder: Poonam, can you get *me* one more *parantha* , please?

Poonam: You will get late for the shop.

Mrs Arora: *Arre,* what will happen if he is five minutes late. Papaji is already there in the shop. Ravinder is a growing boy. Go and make another *parantha* for him.

Poonam: But, but...1 thought you said ...

Mrs Arora: (threateningly) What did I say?

Poonam: No, nothing, Mummyji.

Ravinder: Dearest, I know you don't want me to get fat, but I promise you, I'll reduce my intake from tomorrow.

(Poonam *goes* into the kitchen.)

Mrs Arora: What did her mother say yesterday ?

Ravinder: Gulshan will *come* with a draft of Rupees two hundred thousand today.

Mrs Arora: Yes, yes. That's old hat, but what about the remaining eight.

Ravinder: Let's encash this draft first, then we can insist on the rest.

Mrs Arora: We can't afford to wait too long. Guptaji was saying that that particular shop is hot property, and it's only because of our close relationship that he hasn't thought of selling it to anyone else. All American multinational company is thinking of grabbing it as a retail outlet for fried chicken.

Ravinder: I know, I know. I'll think of something to pressurise her.

Mrs Arora: You keep on thinking. Like your Papaji. Before that I'll do something.

(Poonam returns carrying a plate with a parantha on it.)

Ravinder: Ah, my precious . . ..

Poonam: Here, my dear.

Ravinder: Thank you, *my* dear. Why don't you sit down, dearest ?

(Poonam sits down at the dining table.)

Mrs Arora: I'll go and clean the toilet. The sweeper has done such a poor job ... (pauses meaningfully) and nobody else helps.

Exit Mrs Arora

Ravinder: I'll be back early, my dear . We can see the matinee show. Be dressed Beforehand , will you ?

Poonam: Of course, dear.

Ravinder: (standing up) All right then. I am off to the shop. Give me a kiss now.

(Poonam kisses Ravinder)

Exit Ravinder

(Poonam starts clearing the table. In a while, the bell chimes. Poonam goes to open the door.)

Enter Gulshan

Gulshan: Hello, sister.

Poonam: *Bhaiya*!!

Gulshan: How's my darling sister?

Poonam: I am fine, *bhaiya*.

(They embrace)

(Mrs Arora quietly enters in the meanwhile.)

Mrs Arora: Harrumph. What is happening?

Poonam: (separating) Gulshan *bhaiya* has *come*.

Mrs Arora: I can see that I'm not blind (with a leering expression) I can see everything. Come in, Mr Gulshan. Please be seated.

Gulshan: Thank, you, ma'am.

Mrs Arora: Poonam, go and get a glass of water for the guest.

Poonam: Yes, Mummyji.

(She goes to the kitchen to get water)

Mrs Arora: Yes. Mr Gulshan. Have you brought the bank draft with you? Mrs Bajaj told Poonam on the phone yesterday that . . .

Gulshan: (hastily) Oh, yes, I have. (He takes out a draft from his pocket) Here it is.

Mrs Arora: (takes the draft) Please do tell Mrs Bajaj whenever you meet her that this money is certainly not enough for Ravinder to buy the shop he has an eye on. Why, for this money you couldn't even get a shop in *Kabadi bazaar,* could you?

Gulshan: If you like, I could find out the prevailing rales at *Kabadi bazaar*.

Mrs Arora: What on earth for? Are you out of your mind, Mr Gulshan? Do you for a moment imagine that Ravinder is going to setup his business in that disgusting , filthy place? By the way, have you washed your hands?

Gulshan: Oh, yes, madam.

Mrs Arora: When?

Gulshan: When?

Mrs Arora: Yes, I mean how much time ago.

Gulshan: Well, in the morning I suppose.

Mrs Arora: I didn't think you had stepped out of your house without even having washed your hands. So you haven't washed them after you left *Kabadi bazaar?*

Gulshan: No, I guess not.

Mrs Arora: You would do me a big favour if you wash them once more. The bathroom straight ahead.

Gulshan: (reluctantly) All right, madam, If you insist.

(He goes into the washroom to wash his hands. Mrs Arora examines the draft very minutely, and then satisfied, she puts it away and then starts dusting the furniture. Gulshan returns shortly.)

Mrs Arora: (a little suspiciously) Have you washed them properly?

Gulshan: (embarrassed) Oh, yes, Auntyji, although it wasn't really necessary.

Mrs Arora: Don't say that. The diseases one can catch in that area can be really infectious.

Gulshan: Yes, but I don't suppose . ...

(Poonam enters carrying tea and biscuits on a tray.)

Poonam: *Bhaiya,* I hope you are going to stay for lunch.

Gulshan: Well...

Mrs Arora: No, of course he can't stay for lunch. He has to attend to his shop, don't you, Gulshan?

Gulshan: Well...

Mrs Arora: No need to be polite. You finish your tea and then rush back to your shop.

Gulshan: All right , Auntyji.

Poonam: Have some biscuits, *bhaiya*?

Mrs Arora: Go ahead and eat a biscuit, Gulshan. These are from the best bakery in Princes Market.

(takes a biscuit and gulps down his tea.)

Gulshan: I think I will take your leave now, Auntyji.

Poonam: Come again, *bhaiya*.

Gulshan: I'll come by in another four, five days.

Poonam: Do that.

Exit Gulshan

Mrs Arora: Now that he has gone, perhaps the Maharani can get down to some housework.

Poonam: Mummyji , what shall I do?

Mrs Arora: You can start by sweeping the carpet, and be sure to clean all the dust which has gathered below it as well.

Poonam: Mummyji,, I can't do this work.

Mrs Arora: Why ever not? Is it below the dignity of this Maharani to sweep *carpets*?

Poonam: I didn't mean that, Mummyji. It's just that I'm very allergic to carpet dust.

Mrs Arora: (suspiciously) Allergic to carpet dust! It's the first time I heard of such a thing. I hope you haven't brought any other allergies and diseases from your house.

Poonam: (contritely) No, Mummyji.

Mrs Arora: (thinks for a while). In that case you can clean up all the fans in the house today.

Poonam: All the fans, Mummyji.

Mrs Arora: Yes, of course. Can't you see that the fans all over the house have turned black with dust? I am too old to clean them now. Today, you can do only this much that you can clean up all the fans in the house.

Poonam: Mummyji, today we were thinking of going out ....

Mrs Arora: Going out! Today? Whatever for? Certainly not !Go out some other day. Not today.

Poonam: All right, Mummyji.

Mrs Arora: Why don't you start right away? You are so short that you wouldn't be able to reach the fans. See that stool. You can stand on it.

Poonam: As you say. Mummyji.

Mrs Arora: I'm going to get some rest. Oh my legs ....

(Poonam takes hold of the stool and begins cleaning the fan in the drawing room. After she has finished, she gets down from the stool and sits down glumly on the sofa. The needles of the wall clock now move to show that time has passed and it is now two thirty. There is the sound of chimes to show that a half hour has passed.)

(Enter Ravinder)

Ravinder: Hullo, hullo. What is this? I told you, my dear. that you should be dressed and waiting when I came to collect you for the movie. You haven't even changed your nightdress Now, the tickets will go waste. Why aren't you ready?

Poonam: (sullenly) Ask your mother.

Ravinder: All right. I will ask her. What is the meaning of all this? (shouts) Mummyji.

(Poonam leaves the drawing room and goes into the adjoining bedroom. Mrs Arora re-enters the drawing room.)

Mrs Arora: Yes, my son. What is it? What has happened? Why are you so excited?

Ravinder: Mother, I was to go to the cinema with Poonam today. She's not dressed and seems to be in a bad mood. Have you said something to her?

Mrs Arora: Tell me, my son, are movies more important to you or this shop which you want to buy?

Ravinder: Obviously the shop, mother.

Mrs Arora: Well, then, take this draft and deposit it in the bank at once. What have you discussed with Guptaji?

Ravinder: He says that with a four hundred thousand rupee cash advance we can go ahead and sign the agreement any time I wish to. The balance would have to be paid within two months, so we have some time.

Mrs Arora: How much money have you and Papaji arranged for?

Ravinder: About one hundred thousand.

Mrs Arora: Here is a draft for two hundred thousand. This means that there is still a shortfall of one hundred thousand.

Ravinder: That's right, mother.

Mrs Arora: Can't we persuade Guptaji to settle for a three hundred thousand cash advance.

Ravinder: I'll try, but I don't think he will agree. The problem is mother that we can't raise any more money from the market at this stage. Once we have Guptaji's signature on the agreement, we should be able to raise a million rupees.

Mrs Arora: In that case, you tell Poonam that her mother should arrange for one hundred thousand more at the earliest.

Ravinder: (agrees) I'll talk to her. Listen, mother I think you are being too harsh on her. Take it easy.

Mrs Arora: One can't be easy. You don't understand these kinds of people, my son. They understand only one language.

Ravinder: No, mother, you are being too harsh. They are weak, timid souls. They will pay. Don't worry. I know how to handle them.

Mrs Arora: All right. I'll cool down for a day or so. That stupid Pujari fooled us. We should have investigated the family more thoroughly.

Ravinder: Don't blame yourself, Mummy. What else could we have done?

Mrs Arora: Engaged a lawyer, and had the land records checked.

Ravinder: For what?

Mrs Arora: To have made sure that they owned at least the Model Town house.

Ravinder: Who does this Mummy? You are worrying unnecessarily. I'm sure they own the house. They did say it was not rented. I'll push to the bank now, mother. Just take it easy with this girl for a few days.

Exit Ravinder

(Mrs Arora goes into the kitchen briefly, and then goes across to the couple's bedroom carrying a pot of tea on a tray. She finds Poonam there, standing on the bed, cleaning the fan.)

Mrs Arora: Sit down, my dear. Have a break.

Poonam: All right, Mummyji. If you say so.

Mrs Arora: I didn't mean that you should clean up all the fans in the house today itself. Here, drink some tea.

(In a very patient manner, Mrs Arora makes Poonam a cup of tea.)

Poonam: (sipping tea) Thank you, Mummyji.

Mrs Arora: (in a friendly tone) *Beta.* why didn't you tell me that you were to go to the cinema with Ravinder. There would have been no problem in that case. Now poor Ravinder has gone away in a temper.

Poonam: The house cleaning is also important. Mummyji.

Mrs Arora: Listen, *beta,* when I am angry sometimes, don't take things amiss. Quite often, I myself don't realise what I am saying. Understand.

Poonam: Yes, Mummyji.

Mrs Arora: You see, there is so much of work in this house, and there is no one to do it except you and me. All this work would be greatly reduced if we kept a servant. We could keep a servant if the income rose. Now I just hope and pray that Ravinder manages to get hold of this shop and then once the income rises we can afford to keep a servant. Then you and I don't have to slave so much.

Poonam: Yes, Mummyji.

Mrs Arora: All right, my dear. I'll go and say my prayers now. You too take some rest now. You have done enough for the day.

Exit Mrs Arora

(The stage darkens.The clock's needles move to show that it is now ten at night. There is a chiming sound. Poonam is sitting up in bed waiting for Ravinder.)

Enter Ravinder

Ravinder: Hullo, hullo. What is my sweetheart doing? Waiting up for me?

Poonam: Where did you go off without saying anything?

Ravinder: What did you expect? I had to go and return the tickets else the money would have been wasted.

Poonam: I'm sorry, dear.

Ravinder: No, it wasn't your fault. I think mother must have forbidden you. Was it something like that?

Poonam: (hesitantly) Well, it was actually a misunderstanding. Let's not talk about it.

Ravinder: You wanted to see a movie.. didn't you? Tonight I have brought a movie home.

Poonam: You mean we can watch a video? There are so many movies on cable TV as well. It's not the same as watching a movie on the big screen, Ravinder.

Ravinder: My sweetheart, you don't understand .This is a special kind of movie that husband and wife can watch after they are married. We cannot see this in the cinema hall.

Poonam: What kind of movie is that?

Ravinder: Wait and see.

(Ravinder puts in the video into the player. The television is facing them, and the audience cannot see the screen. A sound comes on.)

Ravinder: I'll put the volume down, so that nobody can hear.

Poonam: Are we going to watch a silent film?

Ravinder: No, no. Just give me two minutes to get the right channel for videos. Yes, that's it. Now just lie down on the bed and relax.

Poonam: Okay

(Poonam lies down on the bed. In a while, Ravinder joins her there. They are facing the audience; the TV's back is facing the audience. They watch silently for five minutes, with occasional exclamations from Poonam)

Ravinder: (enjoying himself) You're shocked, aren't you?

Poonam: Shocked ? No, but it's fun. This is a blue movie. Why didn't you tell me it was a blue movie?

Ravinder: (it's his turn to be shocked now) You mean you know about blue movies.

Poonam: Know about them? Of course! Who doesn't, my dear?

Ravinder: And have you seen any?

Poonam: I have.

Ravinder: Ah ha. I keep forgetting you from Delhi.

Poonam: It's nothing to do with being from Delhi silly. I sure the girls in Ghaziabad are also watching.

Ravinder: So what do you think about this one?

Poonam: I feel shy watching them with you.

Ravinder: (reassured) These foreigners really know how to enjoy themselves.

Poonam: Yes, completely shameless, aren't they? I prefer the other ones though.

Ravinder: (interested) Which ones?

Poonam: The ones that have a bit of a story to them. You know they meet at a party or on the beach, there is some romance and then gradually things develop. This video must be from Germany.

Ravinder: How do you know this?

Poonam: In German videos there is no story line. They go straight to the...

Ravinder: I see what you mean, but that's what you want to see don't you?

Poonam: Well, you boys are different, I suppose. For me it seems just like a machine pumping away.

Ravinder: Don't be so fussy. Look at that blonde.

Poonam: (shyly) She is beautiful, isn't she?

Ravinder: Such big breasts.

Poonam: And look at that man. dear.

Ravinder: What about him?

Poonam: Such a big organ.

Ravinder: (embarrassed) Yes

Poonam: Is it for real? Do they really come that big?

Ravinder: Yes, of course. Now keep quiet and watch.

(After a while)

Ravinder: I'll get some of those slow video's next time if you like those more.

Poonam: Yes, these are so mechanical aren't they ? (suddenly excited) Can you get some with animals.

Ravinder: With animals? You watched videos with animals?!

Poonam: Only two or three. My favourite...

Ravinder: Yes, which is your favourite.

Poonam: It's one with a gorilla. I really got excited with that one.

Ravinder: A gorilla! My God! How many blue movies have you watched?

Poonam: Well, you know Gulshan *bhaiya* used to..

Ravinder: (interrupting furiously) You've watched blue movies with Gulshan *bhaiya*.

Poonam: Speak softly. Mummyji Papaji will hear.

Ravinder: (angrily) You've watched blue movies with Gulshan *bhaiya*...

Poonam: No, no. I used to watch them with Madhu *didi*.

Ravinder: (switches off the video) Then why did vou mention Gulshan *bhaiya's* name just now.

Poonam: I was going to say Gulshan *bhaiya* used to get us the movies.

Ravinder: And you and your Madhu *didi* used to watch?

Poonam: Yes, yes.

Ravinder: (pacified) I see.

Poonam: Now, give me a kiss. You're spoiling all the effects of the movie.

(Ravinder gives her a kiss)

Scene 7

(The house of the Arora's . Mrs Arora is lying on the sofa in the drawing room and wailing about how her legs are paining her. Poonam is busy dusting. A dressed up Ravinder rushes past. He stops to say something to Poonam.)

Ravinder: (whispers in Poonam's ear) Last night was wonderful, wasn't it?

Poonam: (blushing) Sssh. Mummyji's watching.

(From the *sofa,* Mrs Arora is watching in anger and with some suspicion)

Ravinder: (straightening up) Bye, Poonam. Bye, Mummyji.

Mrs Arora: Why are you getting up so late everyday, son? Mr Gupta will be waiting at the shop, won't he?

Ravinder: Oh, but Mummy, Papaji is there at the shop.

Mrs Arora: (scornfully) Papaji ?! Do you think he can handle Guptaji? A seasoned man like him. A man like him will take your father's trousers off in two minutes and your Papaji wouldn't even have realised what is happening.

Ravinder: I get your point, mother. Don't worry. I'll be there in five minutes.

Mrs Arora: Call from the shop to let me know how things develop.

Exit Ravinder

(Mrs Arora gets back to the sofa and her leg complaining. Poonam carries on with the dusting. In a few minutes the front door bell rings.)

Mrs Arora: (opens the door cautiously, espies Mr Gupta) Oh, Mr Gupta! Welcome! Welcome! What a pleasant surprise.

Mr Gupta: (a frail, sick looking man dressed conservativelv in a Nehru jacket) I was passing this way and I thought I may find Ravinder and Papaji at home only.

Mrs Arora: Oh, no, Ravinder *beta* has only just now gone to the shop and Papaji has been there since the morning. They were supposed to meet you there, weren't they?

Mr Gupta: (looking at his watch) That's right. We are supposed to meet there in another twenty minutes. I thought. I might catch them at home. Sometimes one can talk these matters over better at home. There's more privacy, fewer interruptions from customers, if you know what I mean. (sighs regretfully) Oh, well . . .I'd better be getting along then.

Mrs Arora: No, no, how can you go away like this? (simpering) Tell me, are you only Papaji's friend, not mine. At least sit for two minutes.

Mr Gupta: No, I'd better be getting along.

Mrs Arora: Come on Guptaji, why do you act like a stranger sometime? And why did you and dear Sumitra not come for Ravinder's wedding?

Mr Gupta: (after a significant pause) Oh, that ...I wasn't feeling well enough, *bahenji.*

Mrs Arora: At least have a cup of tea before you leave.

Mr Gupta: Well. . . if you insist. I will just have a quick cup of tea and be on my way.

Enter Mr Gupta

Mr Gupta: (taking a chair) I must say you have a beautiful house, (repeats) A beautiful house !

Mrs Arora: Come on, Guptaji. Your house is even grander. (shouts) Poonam, stop that dusting now. Go into the kitchen and make a cup of tea for Guptaji.

Poonam: (does a polite *Namaste* to Guptaji) Yes, Mummyji.

Mrs Arora: (telling Poonam) . . And also get those dry fruits kept in the corner, (turns to address Guptaji) Guptaji, forgive me for saying this, but you are a *pucca* businessman. You know us for so long. You should give us some concession on this shop deal.

Mr Gupta: If it was in my powers I would certainly have done so.

Mrs Arora: (laughs sarcastically) Leave it Guptaji. If it's not in your power, then in whose power is it? At least give us some time to make the final payment.

Mr Gupta: (rubbing his temples) I can't do that *bahenji.* You see I have so many anxieties.

Mrs Arora: (commiserating) What is the matter? I hope you are keeping well.

Mr Gupta: Up and down. High blood pressure, diabetes. The doctor tells me that I should not worry so much.

(Poonam comes in with a pot of tea and a plate full of biscuits and dry fruits)

Mr Gupta: (addressee Poonam, who is making his tea for him) Only a small drop of milk, my dear. No, no sugar at all my dear. I have diabetes, you see. And no cashew nuts. They are salted, aren't they? Oh, they aren't? Well, in that case I'll have a couple. (takes the cup of tea and sips appreciatively) This tea is very good. Thank you, my dear. (turns to Mrs Arora) You see, *bahenji,* my chief anxiety is over the marriage of my daughter Sumitra I think she must be your daughter in law's age. (turns to Poonam) You must come over to our house and meet her sometime, *beta.*

Poonam: Yes, Uncleji.

Mrs Arora: (tactfully) Poonam *beta,* I think there is some dusting to be done in the kitchen as well.

(Poonam leaves)

Mr Gupta: As you know one of Sumitra's legs is a trifle shorter than the other and she walks with a slight limp.

For that reason it may not be easy to find her a good boy, but I will not spare any effort. I am going to give the groom a prince's dowry. A prince's dowry, I repeat! Nothing less than five million

Mrs Arora: (astounded) Five million, did you say?

Mr Gupta: That's right. Five million. Now I already have three million in cash and securities, but the rest of it is all tied up in real estate. That's why I'm in a hurry to sell off this shop for two million. I know perfectly well I will get three million in another three months. The rates are sure to climb with the arrival of multinationals. However, I cannot afford to wait. You understand now why I cannot give you more time to make the payment.

Mrs Arora: (repeats, savouring the words) Five million rupees !

Mr Gupta: You see, I have decided to give the boy who marries Sumitra five million now, because in any case Sumitra will inherit everything after I have gone. You know Sumitra my only child. The trend is changing now. People now say that one should give away part of one's wealth while one is still alive, so that others can enjoy it while they are young. Now who knows how many years more I have left.

Mrs Arora: Oh, don 't say that Guptaji. You have many years left. I'm sure you'll survive us all.

Mr Gupta: That's kind of you to say so.

Mrs Arora: I suppose you're looking for a rich business family, or someone with an industry.

Mr Gupta: No, no. I'm not looking for a rich family.

Mrs Arora: No?! Why ever not?

Mr Gupta: If it's a really rich family, five million will mean nothing for them. The richer people are, the greedier they get . I know this from my experience.

Mrs Arora: Yes , you're right. Now-a-days, people are so greedy.

Mr Gupta: In earlier times, people were not so obsessed with money. What could you buy with money? There were no goods. There were so few things to buy. Hardly anyone owned a car in those days. I tell you, even thirty years ago, there were less than a hundred people in Ghaziabad who owned a car. If you owned one, even a third rate second hand model, you were someone of stature and position in the city. Now, everyone has a Maruti. Even someone with a stall selling *pan* and cigarettes has one. There are so many goods to buy in the market. Music systems, video's, washing machines, you name it. So people have become greedy.

Mrs Arora: You're right, you're right It's terrible how greedy some people have become. And deceitful as well.

Mr Gupta: I sometimes go to your shop just to talk with Papaji. Such a good hearted and simple soul, your husband is. You hardly find anyone like him these days.

Mrs Arora: That's true, that's so true.

Mr Gupta: And that is why the family too is so good...

Mrs Arora: Oh Guptaji, you flatter us so.

Mr Gupta: No, no, not at all. It is an indicator of the other members of the family, how one member of the family is, particularly the head of the family. Anyhow, what I was really trying to say was that the old values have gone. Nowadays, everybody is money minded, everybody is a consumer. You understand me, madam?

Mrs Arora: Yes, yes. Of course.

Mr Gupta: It's only when this age old practice of dowry combines with modern consumerism that the resulting concoction makes for a deadly cocktail. Do you agree, madam?

Mrs Arora: I don't understand exactly what you are saying, Guptaji, but I do agree with you. You are so intelligent.

Mr Gupta: Not at all, madam, not at all. You are the intelligent one. I'm so happy to have had this chance to talk to you today

Mrs Arora: Forgive me Guptaji, but I think you are unnecessarily worried.

Mr Gupta: Yes?

Mrs Arora: If you are going to give five million, five *million,* then I think any family, even a rich one, will always appreciate that fact.

Mr Gupta: After some time a rich family will forget about the five million dowry... and they might start thinking then that after all Sumitra is a handicapped person.

Mrs Arora: Oh, they wouldn't. Not with that kind of money.

Mr Gupta: Yes, they will. I'm telling you. It's a matter of psychology. Now, on the other hand if I marry Sumitra off to a poor family, it will also not be a wise decision . They will have a different approach to life, a different way of thinking from ours, and they will be an embarrassment for me in front of my relatives. It will also not be easy for Sumitra to adjust in such a family.

Mrs Arora: Then who will you marry her off to?

Mr Gupta: A middle class family who will properly appreciate what five million means. They will never be able to forget the difference the money made to their lifestyles. The possibilities it gave them. Sumitra will live like a queen in that house.

Mrs Arora: Why, you will be able to get the best of boy's for that kind of money.

Mr Gupta: I'm not so sure. These days good boys are very hard to come by. Take your own son Ravinder. Where do you find boys like him these days?! Find me someone like him and I will immediately fix up my daughter's marriage.

Mrs Arora: Someone like Ravinder. You mean . . . (blurts out) Oh, why didn't you tell us earlier, Guptaji? (has a sudden realisation) So that is why you and Sumitra dear didn't turn up for Ravinder's wedding!

Mr Gupta: (it's his turn to look surprised now) But I thought you people were not interested. Sumitra *beti* would have been very happy with a boy like Ravinder. I had even indirectly indicated my keenness to this match to Papaji on several occasions, but he did not give me any response.

Mrs Arora: (looking terribly frustrated) *Arre,* Guptaji. Papaji is a complete simpleton in such matters. He must simply not have understood what you were getting at. Oh, what a shame this is!(pauses) Didn't you ever broach the subject with Ravinder?

Mr Gupta: No, of course not. Some matters are initially discussed only amongst the elders in the family. Of course I never mentioned it to Ravinder. It wouldn't have been proper to do so before I had obtained yours and Papaji's consent. I thought Papaji is not very keen because perhaps Ravinder wants a very beautiful girl as his life partner, since he is such a good looking lad himself (lowers his voice). That is why I was amazed to see your daughter in law. Forgive me for saying so, but I think Sumitra is a shade prettier than your Poonam, did you say her name was?

Mrs Arora: (in a sad tone) Anyhow, bygones are bygones, Guptaji. But I do wish you had given just a hint to me even once. Things would have been totally different.

Mr Gupta: (nodding his head) I realising that now. It's amazing that Papaji didn't get my hints. *See,* had Mrs Gupta been alive, she would have spoken to you. That would have been the proper course of action. Well, I'll be taking your leave now. Ravinder and Papaji will be waiting for me at the shop.

Mrs Arora: (stands up) Well, all right, I guess (goes to the door to see him off) Tell me Guptaji, will you accept a widower for Sumitra?

Mr Gupta: (thoughtful) Well, yes, as long as he is a young fellow, and there are no children from the first marriage. Why, do you have somebody in mind?

Mrs Arora: No.. It's just that I was thinking . . .

Mr Gupta: (folds his hands) All right, *bahenji. namaste.* It was a real pleasure talking to you.

Mrs Arora: (also folds her hands) All right, *bhaisahab namaste.*

Exit Mr Gupta

Mrs Arora: Oh, that stupid fool, Papaji. I could murder him for this. Such a wonderful proposal for dear Ravinder had come our way, and it has slipped out of our hands. And instead of dear Sumitra we have got this silly bitch that is just interested who hasn't even brought some decent jewellery with her. (addresses the audience) I doubt if we could pawn it off for more than a hundred thousand.

(Poonam comes in from the kitchen)

Poonam: I've finished with dusting the kitchen, Mummyji. Has Gupta uncle gone? What's happening about the shop? (sees Mrs Arora's face) What's wrong Mummyji. You look positively unwell.

Mrs Arora: Look who's asking? The cause of it all. My headaches, my tensions, my worries . . . (Just then the bell rings) Who can it be now? (goes to the door and opens it cautiously)

Enter Gulshan

Mrs Arora: Oh, it's you ! Again!! Why have you come?

Gulshan: Auntyji, I was just passing this way . . .

Mrs Arora: Passing this way? Why. does our house fall on the way to Kabadi bazaar Passing this way indeed !

Poonam: (joyfully) Gulshan *bhaiya*!! How nice of you to come.

Mrs Arora: (with obvious reluctance) Well, come on in. Don't just stand at the door like a sweeper. Come in and sit. Poonam, you look after Mr Gulshan. I'm going to rest. I have splitting headache.

(Mrs Arora picks up the plate of dry fruit kept on the table in a surreptitious manner, and goes and keeps it in the kitchen. She then goes off to the adjoining bedroom).

Mrs Arora: (muttering to herself) At least from here I can keep an eye on them. I hope she doesn't go and bring the dry fruit from the kitchen for her *kabadia* brother.

(Mrs Arora lies down on the bed, usually occupied by Ravinder and Poonam.)

Gulshan: I hope I haven't come at the wrong time.

Poonam: No, no, *bhaiya.* It's so nice that you've come (softly) and it is good that she's gone off to sleep. We can talk more freely.

Gulshan: What's biting Auntyji?

Poonam: Oh, just ignore whatever she says. Ravinder says she is very moody. Half the time she herself doesn't realise what she is saying. Don't mind what she says.

Gulshan: Oh, if that's the case, then I guess it's all right. I was worrying about you.

Poonam: Yes, yes, she is just like that. Don't worry.

Gulshan: All right. But tell me about yourself. How is my darling sister getting along?

Poonam: (is quiet for a minute) I'm absolutely fine *bhaiya..* Just missing home a bit, like all girls do.

Gulshan: And how are you getting alongwith your dear husband. That's the main thing.

Poonam: He is very good. And even Papaji is simply wonderful (lowers her voice) Only Mummyji is a bit funny at times. It's best to ignore her, Ravinder says. Have some biscuits, *bhaiya.* I'll just get some dry fruit. Just now the plate was here.

Gulshan: Don't bother, my dear sister. These biscuits are fine. Tell me, your mother in law isn't troubling you on account of dowry, is she?

Poonam: Well, *bhaiya* . . . (suddenly exclaims) Oh' Something has gone into my eye.

Gulshan: (whips out his handkerchief in a flash) Don't move. I'll have it out in a jiffy.

(Meanwhile in the bedroom, Mrs Arora is tossing and turning in the bed.)

Mrs Arora: (muttering to herself) I can't get any sleep, it's because of this girl, I think. Every since she's come, I don't know what has happened to my sleep, (suddenly very alert) Strange! I can't hear any voices any more. That fellow Gulshan couldn't have gone so soon. I hope he has. I hope she hasn't given him the dry fruits to eat. Let me go and check.

(She opens the bedroom door a bit and peers out. Meanwhile Gulshan is removing the speck of dust from Poonam's eye)

Gulshan: Don'l move, my dear. You know I an expert in such tasks.

(Mrs Arora pushes open the bedroom door now, and strides out furiously)

Mrs Arora: (loudly) What? What? What is this happening?

Gulshan: Nothing, Auntyji. I was just.

Mrs Arora: Silence, you rascal! I have seen everything. Don't you try and pretend innocence with me. I go to the bedroom for a minute and you immediately start kissing this sex crazed bitch.

Poonam: (almost in tears now) Mummyji, it's not what you think. Gulshan was just ...

Mrs Arora: So now it's Gulshan, is it. Not even Gulshan *bhaiya*. *Arre,* you shameless hussy. I go to my room for two seconds and both of you grab each other like two sex crazed fiends. If he can kiss you even while I am in the house, then what will happen one day if l am not there. You'll take him directly to the bedroom, won't you?

Poonam: (crying) Mummyji, at least listen to us.

Mrs Arora: (shouting at the top other voice now) That's what I've been asking myself. Where has she learnt all her tricks from? (in a harsh, interrogative tone) Since when has this been going on? You bitch! You whore!

Gulshan: (in a disgusted, angry tone) Auntyji, you cannot talk to Poonam like this.

Mrs Arora: (screams) This is my house and I will talk to both of you just as I like. (turns to Poonam) Get out, you bitch. you whore. Get out of this house, this instant. You and your filthy lover from *Kabadi bazaar.*

(Exit a weeping Poonam with an unhappy and perturbed looking Gulshan)

Mrs Arora: Good riddance! Now, I will have a good sleep, (goes to her bedroom and promptly falls asleep)

(The hour hand on the wall clock moves forward by an hour. There is a chiming sound. The front doorbell is ringing. Mrs Arora gets up from her slumber and goes to admit a tired and angry looking Ravinder)

Enter Ravinder

Ravinder: (upset) Mother, what have you been up to now?

Mrs Arora: What have I been up to, he asks? Why don't you ask me what your dear wife has been up to. I caught her kissing that *kabadia* Gulshan, the moment my face was turned.

Ravinder: (quietly) That's not true, mother.

Mrs Arora: Did they come to your shop, son?

Ravinder: (shakes his head) No, mother. From here they went straight to Gulshan's shop in *Kabadi bazaar*. Gulshan telephoned me from his shop and spoke to me. Poonam was in no condition to talk and right now they are both on their way to Delhi. Gulshan says he was just trying to take out a speck of dust from Gulshan's eye . . . and you completely misunderstood the whole scene. I mean you didn't actually see them kiss mouth to mouth, did you ? You just saw him bending over her. He was trying to take out the speck with his handkerchief.

Mrs Arora: I tell you, my son, you are such an innocent person in these matters. I don't know what to say. All can say is that this girl is sexually very experienced.

Ravinder: How can you say that so confidcntly, mother?

Mrs Arora: Well, both of you are in the bedroom all the time, so she has obviously learnt many tricks from many places.

Ravinder: (thoughtful) Yes. there is something in what you say there.

Mrs Arora: Anyhow, there was another very good reason I wanted to get rid of her.

Ravinder: Why did you want to do that. Mother ?

Mrs Arora: We need another hundred thousand rupees to pay Guptaji, don't we? Where is all that money going to come from? Now with this girl gone, we can take out her jewellery from the cupboard and pawn it off. (sniffs) Should be able to get a hundred thousand for it, I think.

Ravinder: (hesitates) Well, alright . . . but there was no need for this mother. We could have got the money out from Poonam's mother. I was in any case planning to go down tomorrow to Delhi to tell her the situation.

Mrs Arora: And supposing she doesn't give you the money? Why won't she, Mother ? She can easily raise the money. Didn't Mr Pujari say that apart from the twenty million house she is living in, she also owns a factory worth thirty million.

Mrs Arora: Who knows, my son? Who knows? Personally I'm no longer so sure she even owns that house in Model Town. There is something fishy here.

Ravinder: (surprised) What makes you say that, mother?

Mrs Arora: Listen, the amount of pressure I've put on her daughter, if she did in fact own that house, she would have coughed up the money by now.

Ravinder: You mean they've pulled one over us (rubs his chin thought fully) I see what you mean. Yes, it is a bit surprising, (thinks hard) All right mother, here's what we'll do. You go ahead and pawn the jewellery so we can pay Mr Gupta the full-agreed advance tomorrow evening. Meanwhile I'll try and get the money out of that old woman tomorrow morning. I'll find out for certain if she does in fact own that house and the factory. Here's what I'll do. (whispers for a while to his mother)

Mrs Arora: (listens carefully) All right. That sounds like a good plan, but if for some reason we can't get the money out other, here's what we'll do. (whispers back for a few minutes) Agreed?

Ravinder: That's too extreme, mother!

Mrs Arora: My son, you will feel the same when I tell you everything.

Ravinder: What do you want to say?

Mrs Arora: I will tell you when you get back. We can discuss it then. Agreed?

Ravinder: Agreed.

Mrs Arora: One more thing, *beta*. Don't mention anything to Papaji. You know how he is. Completely impractical and useless in all such matters.

Ravinder: What will you tell him about Poonam's not being here tonight?

Mrs Arora: Oh, I'll just say Poonam was missing her house and has gone to spend a couple of days with her mother. No point in telling him anything. He will just be a big nuisance.

Ravinder: (laughs) All right mother.

Mrs Arora: That's like a dear boy.

Scene 8

(The next day morning, the scene open at the Bajaj family house. Mrs Bajaj, Poonam and Gulshan are sitting together in the living room.)

Gulshan: Did you speak to Madhu *didi* last night, Aunty?

Mrs. Bajaj: Of course I did. She would have been here right now but unfortunately the poor girl has an admission matter listed in the meaning in the Supreme Court, but she has promised that she will come as soon as she is free. She says we should take no step till she is here.

Gulshan: Whatever do you, do not send Poonam back to that house. They are filthy people with dirty minds.

Poonam: Don't say that Gulshan *bhaiya*. It is only Mummyji who is greedy and is creating problems. Papaji and Ravinder are just fine.

Mrs Bajaj: Rahney dey. If they were all that fine shouldn't they have at least called by now, to ask forgiveness for Arora *behanji's* behaviour. Both of you have been here since last night. Not a single call from either Papaji or Ravinder. You did speak to Ravinder on the phone, and tell him what had happened, didn't you, Gulshan?

Gulshan: Yes, yes, of course.

Mrs Bajaj: So then what was this response.

Gulshan: He wanted to speak to Poonam. I told him she was too upset to talk to him and under the existing circumstances I was taking her bake to Delhi for the time being.

Mrs Bajaj: Well, then at least Ravinder should have telephoned by now. The whole family seems to be like the mother.

Poonam: No, no, you are wrong. Papaji is very nice. Ravinder is very nice.

Gulshan: (sarcastically) Tell us what you want to do then, dear sister. Go back to this nice family. Shall I take you back?

Poonam: No, no, *bhaiya.* I feel too sacred to go back. The way she looked at us, daggers drawn—as if she wanted to kill us both. (laughs nervously)

Mrs Bajaj: No, there is no question of poonam's going back until and unless they fall on their knees and beg for forgiveness.

Gulshan: Okay, Auntyji, I'd better be getting back to Ghaziabad now. You know I have no one to help me at the shop these days.

Mrs Bajaj: All right, Gulshan dear. I don't know what we would have done without you.

Exit Gulshan

Mrs Bajaj: Madhu was right then. I was in too much of a hurry for your marriage. That stupid Mr Pujari fooled us all. We should have had this family investigated more thoroughly.

Poonam: Don't blame yourself, mother. Ravinder is a fine boy.

Mrs Bajaj: (in a sarcastic tone) Ravinder is a fine boy. Ravinder is a fine boy. After all that has happened she still says that.

(Just then the bell rings)

Enter Ravinder, a large suitcase in his hand

Ravinder: (sets the suitcase down, and falls at Mrs Bajaj's feet) Forgive me, Mummyji please forgive me.

Mrs Bajaj: (flustered) Come, come, son. First at least sit down, my dear boy. There is no question of any forgiveness. You have not committed any fault.

(Poonam rushes sobbing to Ravinder, who envelops her in a bear hug , then releases her gently and takes a seat. Mrs Bajaj is visibly moved by this show of affection, and wipes a tear off her cheek)

Ravinder: I have left my home, Mummyji. Now I will stay here only with you and Poonam. I've brought my clothes in that big suitcase.

Mrs Bajaj: (a bit rattled at this turn of events) You're welcome to, of course, my dear boy, for as long as you like.

Ravinder: I can't think of going back to that house where my mother, my own mother, has behaved so badly with my wife.

Mrs Bajaj: You know *beta* what actually happened was that Gulshan was taking out a speck of. . .

Ravinder: I know all about that from Gulshan already, Mummyji. Please don't make me feel worse than I do already. I know Poonam's character is without blemish. It is my mother's wild imagination that I can't control. Even though she now realises her mistake and is even willing to touch Poonam's feet and beg her forgiveness.

Poonam: What?!

Mrs Bajaj: Really?!

Ravinder: (enthusiastically) Yes, of course. You see yesterday evening both Papaji and I gave her hell. She is a changed woman now . . . but that doesn't matter. I don't want to go back now.

Mrs Bajaj: (anxiously) Don't be in such a hurry, my child. After all they are your parents. All said and done, Mrs Arora is your mother.

Ravinder: From today onwards, only you are my mother, Mummyji.

Mrs Bajaj: (touched) That's all right, *beta,* but what will you do in Delhi?

Ravinder: I will reopen the factory.

Mrs Bajaj: Oh, but *beta,* it's actually owned and managed by Poonam's *chacha* now..

Ravinder: (hiding his feeling of shock at this revelation) Is that so? Well, in that case we can mortgage this house, can't we, and I can start some kind of business in Delhi with that money.

Mrs Bajaj: (visibly embarrassed now) No, we can't do that, my dear, you see this house too doesn't belong to me.

Ravinder: (can't hide his feeling of shock anymore) But, Mummyji, you said . . . you said that this is not a rented accommodation.

Mrs Bajaj: (wearily) That's true my dear. I guess we should have told you earlier. The fact of the matter, you see is that Poonam's father incurred heavy losses and the house now belongs to his elder brother, Poonam's *chachaji,* who bailed out my husband. We can just stay here as long as we wish to.

Ravinder: (sounding disheartened) Well, in that case I suppose we had better be going back.

Mrs Bajaj: I'm not so sure about that, *beta.* You see, my niece Madhu, who is a Supreme Court lawyer . . .

Ravinder: Mummyji. please don't fall into the clutches of these lawyers. I know she happens to be your niece, but even then. You're worried that my mother will mistreat Poonam again, aren't you? Well, you needn't have any fears on that score anymore. My mother is just like a docile animal now, (looks at his mother in law's expression) You don't believe that? Let me get you both to talk to each other on the phone.

Mrs Bajaj: (sounding doubtful) Well, I don't know . . .

Ravinder: (picks up the phone, and dials his residence) (soberly) Hullo, hullo. Who's that? Mummyji? Mummyji, Ravinder here Yes, yes. I perfectly fine. So is Poonam. (addresses Mrs Bajaj) Here, she wishes to speak to you. (hands over the phone to Mrs Bajaj).

Mrs Bajaj: I'll switch *on* the speaker phone so we can all hear the conversation.

Mrs Arora: (her voice comes over the speaker) *Bahenji,* I want to touch your feet and beg your forgiveness. I touch your feet, sister. Please forgive me. I don't know what all I have said to Poonam. Actually, you know I can't see very well. Please say that you have forgiven me.

Mrs Bajaj: Bahenji, we were totally devastated. We simply couldn't believe . . .

Mrs Arora: *Bahenji,* could I speak to my daughter please?

Mrs Bajaj: Well, I'm sorry ...she is a bit upset . . .

Mrs Arora: I understand, I understand. It doesn't matter. I will beg her forgiveness once she reaches home. I will touch her feet too, if she wants me too. Ravinder has explained everything to me. It was all a terrible misunderstanding. She is coming home, isn't she? (pause) Can I speak to Ravinder for a minute?

Ravinder: (takes the receiver, sounding serious) Hullo . . . mother?

Mrs Arora: *Beta,* are you coming home . . .?

Ravinder: Yes, mother, we are coming home.

Mrs Arora: Since the morning I have been cooking a pudding for both of you. Carrot pudding. Poonam's favourite. There is some good news. The gas is almost finished.

Ravinder: (sounds puzzled) The gas is almost finished. What are you saying mother? Do you want me to bring another cylinder on the way?

Mrs Arora: No, no.

Ravinder: Then?

Mrs Arora: All right son, I am putting the phone down now. I need to go to the kitchen. I don't want the *halwa* to get burnt, (puts the phone down).

Ravinder: (puts the receiver down, repeats puzzledly). The gas is almost Finished. This js good news. I don't understand what she means.

Mrs Bajaj: (laughing) I can. *Bahenji* must he meaning that it is good the gas is finishing after the *halwa* is cooked.

Ravinder: (still sounding puzzled) I suppose so . .

Poonam: Yes, what else could she mean?

Ravinder: Well Mummyji, I guess we had better he going hack then.

Mrs Bajaj: What's the hurry, *beta?* Have lunch and go. You can also meet Madhu who should be coming anytime.

Ravinder: No, Mummyji, I see that you have been talking sense. My future is only in Ghaziabad. I must go back and try to arrange another hundred thousand to he paid to Mr Gupta as advance.

Mrs Bajaj: (sounding contrite) I'm sorry son that I can't help you more than I have already.

Ravinder: No, no, Mummyji. You have done more than enough.

Poonam: (excited) Tell me Ravinder, did papaji really give Mummyji a shouting?

Ravinder: Yes of course. Papaji gave her hell. I didn't say anything to her as a result. But you should have told me if my mother bad been misbehaving earlier I would have blown her up.

Mrs Arora: That is what I was telling Poonam. You should tell Ravinder or Papaji if there is ever any problem.

Poonam: Oh, Mummyji's been quite all right before this.

Ravinder: Well, next time there is any such problem just tell me or Papaji. If he doesn't, I'll give her a firing.

Poonam: No, no, Mummyji has generally been quite all right with me up to now.

Ravinder: Yon don't know Papaji He's generally a very quiet person as you very well know, but once he loses his temper, he's quite a tiger. I think Murnmyji's quite scared of him now, after yesterday.

Poonam: (sounding well pleased) Oh, I wish I'd been there to see the scene!

Ravinder: Oh, you'll find Mummyji a completely changed person now, I *can* assure you my dearest. Come, Poonam, now let's go.

Mrs Bajaj: (addressing Poonam) So daughter? How do you feel about going back just now?

Poonam: I'll go back with Ravinder now, otherwise Mummyji will feel bad.

Mrs Bajaj: All right then.

Exeunt Ravinder and Poonam

Mrs Bajaj: (addressing the audience) Well, I hope I have done the right thing. Surely nothing can go wrong now.

The bell rings

Enter Madhu (dressed in her lawyer's robes)

Madhu: (sounding breathless) Hullo, Auntyji. I reached here as soon as I could, (is surprised to see that Mrs Bajaj is all alone) . . . but where are Poonam and Gulshan.

Mrs Bajaj: *Beta,* Gulshan left in the morning and Poonam has only just left with Ravinder.

Madhu: (astonished) Left with Ravinder? Auntyji, what have you done? Didn't I tell you not to take any step till I reached?

Mrs Bajaj: Yes, but we couldn't keep on waiting for you my dear. Ravinder needed to return to Ghaziabad urgently.

Madhu: Oh, well, what's done is done. Tell me what happened. Auntyji, tell me everything that happened after we spoke to each other last night. Don't miss a single word.

Mrs Bajaj: What is there to tell, beta? Mrs Arora has realised her mistake. She was even willing to touch Poonam's feet. (giggles) Imagine! She was so repentant that she has been cooking Poonam's favourite pudding since the morning.

Madhu: (sounds skeptical) Really?! She has been making carrot pudding for Poonam? After the way she behaved yesterday.

Mrs Bajaj: Yes, yes. I'm telling you. Don't be so disbelieving - like a typical lawyer. I heard her myself on the speakerphone. We could hear every word she said to Ravinder.

Madhu: Oh, I see. What did she say exactly?

Mrs Bajaj: (trying to remember) You lawyers always want the exact words, don't you? ...yes, I've got it. She said to him, 'There is good news. The gas has finished while making the *halwa*. What she actually meant to say was that...'

Madhu: (extremely agitated) The gas has finished!? Oh, my God, that's not good news, Auntyji. Thats's terrible. That's horrible. My God! What shall we do?

Mrs Bajaj: (frightened suddenly) What are you saying, Madhu? Everything is perfectly fine.

Madhu: (furious) Every thing is Not perfectly fine (starts shouting). Do you realise what they are planning to do, Auntyji. Auntyji, they are planning to murder our Poonam.

Mrs Bajaj: (shaking now, her earlier confidence all gone) No, no, what are you saying? It can't be . . .

Madhu: (firmly) It is. Yes. That's the plan. I'm pretty sure of it. There is no time to waste now. We have to call the police at once. We have to call the police at once. (goes to the telephone and starts dialling) Hullo, is this the Crime Against Womens Cell,

Nanakpura? Hullo, this is Advocate Madhu speaking. Can I speak to ACP Manjeet Arya? Yes, I'm holding. Hullo. Manjeet. This is Madhu. You remember we met in the Supreme Court today morning. Well, I'm calling in connection with another dowry extortion case. We might need to act fast. I'm calling from the girl's mothers house in Model Town. She's my aunt. Shall we come to Nanakpura? Will you send some policemen with us? It's a Ghaziabad case. All right, all right. I'm just reaching there in half an hour with the girl's mother. She will lodge the formal complaint.

Scene 9

(This *scene takes* place in the Arora house. Poonam and Ravinder have only just returned from Delhi. They ring the bell. Mrs Arora goes to open the door.)

Mrs Arora: (smiling at Poonam) Come, come, *beti*..

Poonam: (touches her mother in law's feet) I hope you're not upset anymore, Mummyji.

Mrs Arora: No, *beta,* not at all. You're the one who might be upset. Come, *beta* Ravinder. Come in and rest for a while, both of you. You must be tired from going up and down.

Ravinder: I'm not tired, Mummyji but Poonam is. She hasn't slept the whole of last night.

Mrs Arora: That's just fine. She should go to sleep immediately.

Poonam: Thank you, Mummyji. I'm really feeling extremely drowsy.

Mrs Arora: Well, then you just go and lie down, beta. I will wake you up soon enough though to eat your favourite *halwa.* After that you can sleep as long as you like (she drawls out the last part of the sentence in a ghoulish fashion).

Poonam: Thanks, Mummyji. Excuse me, please. Poonam goes off to her bedroom.

Mrs Arora: So what is the *news* from your side, Ravinder?

Ravinder: Nothing, mother. It was just as you had guessed. They haven't got a *naya paisa* on them. Even that house doesn't belong to them. Neither the factory. Filthy beggars.

Mrs Arora: And liars too. Never mind, beta. The world is like that. You cannot trust anyone these days. Meanwhile there is some good news. While you were away, I called the jewellers. I have pawned off the girl's jewellery, and managed to get another hundred thousand in order to hold Mr Gupta off. The jewellers came home to assess the jewellery. Imagine. Such paupers. Just gave a hundred thousand rupees worth of jewellery to their own daughter.

Ravinder: I had asked her earlier if we could sell it off and she flatly refused.

Mrs Arora: The selfish bitch! Well, that's why we have to get rid of her.

Ravinder: No, mother, that's too extreme a step.

Mrs Arora: My son, do you want to spend the rest of your life struggling to make two ends meet.

Ravinder: We 're not so badly off, mother.

Mrs Arora: All right, if you say so. You would have been a millionaire today if it hadn't been for your Papaji. (hesitates) Listen son, there is something I must tell you.

Ravinder: Yes, mother.

Mrs Arora: Let me whisper it into your ear, son. The girl may come back.

(Mrs Arora whispers something into Ravinder's ear)

Ravinder: Really, mother! Are you certain?

Mrs Arora: Yes, of course I'm certain. That is why we have to get rid of her today itself, now that we've managed to get her back. When she wakes up and finds out about the jewellery, she is going to create a scene, and will want to go back to her parent's house.

Ravinder: I'm not so sure she will want to do that.

Mrs Arora: (in a very convinced tone) She will. Don't go by that docile act she puts on. We women are like tigers when it comes to our jewellery.

Ravinder: I still think we should wait for a couple of days.

Mrs Arora: No, we have to do it today itself, and now. I've got it all planned out. First, you take this money and buy this large can of kerosene. Just go and get it from the market. The rest I will manage.

Ravinder: I'll help you out mother.

Mrs Arora: No, no. You shouldn't be here, understand. You be at the shop with Papaji. I'll telephone you that an accident has taken place.

Ravinder: Don't be silly. Mummy. I'll stay with you and help out. She's a young girl after all. You won't be able to overpower her on your own.

Mrs Arora: My innocent, darling son. I won't need to overpower her, *beta.* After she's eaten the *ha!wa,* she'll sleep so soundly that even an earthquake won't be able to wake her up. I've mixed some very potent sleeping herbs in her *halwa,* you see.

Ravinder: You're very clever, mother, But in that case why not give her an overdose? Wouldn't it be simpler, and less messy too?

Mrs Arora: Now you're talking like that Mrs Bansal, who had come to consult me last year. but didn't lake my advice. That's what she had done. given an overdose to her daughter in law, in spite of my advice, and now she and her son are both in jail. I telling you, it's not safe, my dear. Don't forget that the Bajaj's have that lawyer bitch as a relative. They will certainly call the police on this issue, and if there is a post-mortem and they get the stomach pumped out, they will immediately know that it was death through poisoning. Where will that leave you and Papaji? Don't argue with me, *beta.* Mother knows best.

Ravinder: All right mother, but I'm just feeling terribly nervous.

Mrs Arora: Don't be nervous, my child fortune favours the brave. God has sent us good omen today. The gas has finished.

Ravinder: You mentioned that in the morning on the phone as well. Why should that be good news, mother.

Mrs Arora: It's simple. The first thing people will enquire will be the reason why the kerosene stove was being used at all. If the gas was running, where was the need?

Ravinder: But couldn't she have got burnt with the gas itself? Why kerosene at all?

Mrs Arora: Ah, that's what you don't understand, these technical details. Accidents are much more probable with kerosene stoves.

Ravinder: You' re brilliant, mother.

Mrs Arora: Now I think you should go and get the kerosene.

Ravinder: All right mother. I'll just pop off to the market and get it.

(Just then the telephone starts ringing.

Ravinder: (picks up the receiver) It could be Guptaji's phone. Let me attend this. (speaks into the instrument) Hullo, hullo.

(Mrs Arora presses the speakerphone button. Papaji's voice fills the room.)

Papaji: Hullo, hullo. Is that Ravinder *beta*.

Ravinder: Yes, Papaji

Papaji: I didn't see you in the morning, son. Your mother told me you'd gone off to Delhi early in the morning.

Ravinder: (in a careful tone) Yes, Papaji. That's right.

Papaji: Is dear Poonam still staying with her mother?

Ravinder: No, Papaji. I've brought her back with me.

Papaji: listen son, your mother told me last night that Poonam was missing her home very much and had gone to be with her mother for two, three days.

Ravinder: (very careful now) That is right, Papaji.

Papaji:	I have a feeling that your mother may not be telling the full truth. She may have been misbehaving with dear Poonam.
Ravinder:	(innocently) No, Papaji. In that case Poonam would surely have told me so.
Papaji:	She's a very innocent child. She would not want to create a scene in the house.
Ravinder:	But Papaji why should mother treat her badly? Why should she do that?
Papaji:	You know son, she's very keen on your new shop, and she may be pressurising Bajaj *behnji* to give some more money, I'm afraid you don't know your mother as well as I do. son. I tell you what I'll do. I'll just come home and the two of us will have a heart to heart chat wilh Pooiiam *beti,* and try and find out what's been happening in the house between your mother and her in our absence.
Ravinder:	(hastily) No, no, Papaji. don't do that. Someone needs to be at the shop. In any case she's sleeping right now. I'll talk to her when she wakes up.
Papaji:	All right, son. Be very gentle with her.
Ravinder:	Of course. Papaji.
Papaji:	Shall I come down in, say an hour's time, as well.
Ravinder:	No, Papaji, you just stay at the shop, and come at your regular time in the evening. We don't want to lose any business, do we?
Papaji:	All right, son. There's a customer who's just entered the shop. Let me attend to him.
Ravinder:	Yes. Papaji.
Papaji:	Don't tell your mother any of what I've just told you. After all I could be completely off mark, and maybe your mother is not so bad after all.
Ravinder:	No, of course not Papaji. You know me better than that. Bye now.

Papaji: Bye.

(Ravinder puts down the receiver)

Mrs Arora: (boiling) that spineless weakling!!

Ravinder: Come on Mummyji. Take it easy.

Mrs Arora: Gumless! Spineless !! He's of no use to a woman.

Ravinder: Come on Mummyji. Relax.

Mrs Arora: No, he's taking her side, the fool.

Ravinder: Let's think of what we have to do now.

Mrs Arora: (pulling herself together with some effort) I'm so glad you aren't like your father.

Ravinder: I was going to get the kerosene.

Mrs Arora: Oh. yes.

Ravinder: Okay then, I'll just be back in a short while.

Exit Ravinder

(Mrs Arora now goes into the kitchen, puts some *halwa* on a plate, and goes to the bedroom where Poonam is sleeping. She gently nudes Poonam awake.)

Poonam: (groggily) Hullo ? Where am I ? Mummyji ?

Mrs Arora: Here beta, have some of this *halwa* and then go right back to sleep. No one will disturb you.

Poonam: (warmly) Mummyji, you are being so nice to me (starts eating) It's delicious, Mother! It has wonderful flavours. You must teach me how to cock it like this.

Mrs Arora: Of course, my darling, (makes a face at the audience, which Poonam does not see)

(Poonam eats the *halwa* and promptly goes back to sleep. Mrs Arora waits for a while to make sure Poonam is knocked out.)

Mrs Arora: (mutters triumphantly) Now you will just keep on sleeping, my sleeping ugly.

(Mrs Arora goes back to the drawing room, and lies down on the sofa.)

Enter Ravinder

Ravinder: Here is the kerosene, mother. Five litres, you had said.

Mrs Arora: Oh, yes, my son. That's quite enough. We don't want the house burning down as well, do we? (laughs) Five litres is enough to burn her, and yet keep the house safe. Now there is just one thing left for you to do. Just pick up your wife and put her in the living room next to the kitchen entrance. It must look realistic, you see - that she tried to leave the kitchen an call someone for help.

(Ravinder goes to the bedroom, where he picks up a sleeping Poonam quite easily.)

Poonam: (muttering in her sleep) Not now, Ravinder. I feeling too sleepy. (pause) All right then, go ahead, (pause) You're not doing it? (pause) Well, that's okay as well. Let me sleep then.

(A startled Ravinder carries her to the living room where he dumps her on to the floor next to the kitchen.)

Ravinder: Mother, are you quite sure she won't wake up?

Mrs Arora: Oh, yes, my son.

Ravinder: (anxious) Well, just now she was talking in her sleep.

Mrs Arora: That just goes to show how fast asleep she is. No, she would be completely knocked out. I've given her enough to knock out a horse.

Ravinder: What next, mother?

Mrs Arora: Nothing, my dear. You just go to the shop straight away now. You must have a cast iron alibi. That was the other mistake Mrs Bansal made. Her son was in the house at that time, so now he is in jail as well. See, we must learn from other people's mistakes. Once you are at the shop call the neighbouring shopkeepers to your shop for a small celebration about the new shop you are going to be buying in Princes Market. Then at exactly ten minutes past five-set your watch with the big clock, hanging there-I will call you and tell you -so that everybody else can hear it as well and can be witnesses on our behalf tomorrow if neecssary-that there has been an accident.

Ravinder: I still maintain, mother, even if you set her on fire, she may somehow escape. The bitch is quite strong.

Mrs Arora: No, no, I can handle this. Don't worry. Even if something happens it me, I can risk. it for the sake of my son's future.

Ravinder: Well, mother, if you insist.

Mrs Arora: Go now, and make sure your Papaji stays at the shop only. You never know with him. He may suddenly come home with a stomachache, and then the whole programme will be upset.

Ravinder: All right mother. I'll leave now, if you're sure you don 't need me for anything. If all goes well, then maybe next month when the deal with Guptaji is going to be finalised, you can broach the subject of Sumitra and me.

Mrs Arora: That's right, my clever son. Go now. Don't worry. Everything will go like clockwork.

Ravinder: Best of luck, mother.

Exit Ravinder

Mrs Arora: (mutters to herself) Well, there's nothing to do, but wait for half an hour. I may as well do some dusting in the meanwhile (begins to dust the drawing room tables and chairs desultorily) (suddenly enthusiastic) Wait, let me pour some kerosene over her in the meanwhile. (She takes the can and sprinkles some kerosene liberally over a sleeping Poonam, then puts the can aside in a corner) What shall I do now? (looks at the wall clock) There's still some time to set her alight. That reminds me. This is a good time to dust the carpet, this lazy bitch (looks at a sleeping Poonam) pretended that she had some allergy and refused to clean the carpet. I may as well do that now.

(She fetches a broom from the kitchen and begins swiping the carpet. Some dust flies in Poonam's direction and she sneezes violently)

Poonam: Achoo, achoo, achoo . . . (stands up in order to sneeze properly) acchoo, achoo . . .

(Poonam walks around the room, sneezing violently. A tape recording for two, three minutes could be used to make it sound realistic as well as loud.)

Mrs Arora: Oh, my God. what's happened to her?

Poonam: Achoo achoo. achoo ...

(After a few minutes of sneezing, she comes back and lies down at the same spot closes her eyes and goes back to sleep.)

Mrs Arora: (relieved) Thank goodness.

(Poonam is however quiet only for a few minutes, for once again she gets a sneezing fit.)

Poonam: Achoo, achoo . . . (once again stands up in order to sneeze better, and her bout of sneezing over, she goes back to sit at the same spot.)

Mrs Arora: (folds her hands) Dear God, let her go back to sleep now.

Poonam: (wide awake now) (speaking to herself) Oh, what am I doing here? I should be in my bed. And why do my clothes smell so badly? (She then spots the can of kerosene and a morose looking Mrs Arora sitting beside it, terror stricken from having witnessed this sneezing fit) (She screams violently) *Mummyji*! You are trying to burn me alive. I'll just call Ravinder and tell him what you are up to....

Mrs Arora: Wait, *beta,* wait.

Poonam: (incredulous) Wait for you to kill me off. No way, mother in law. I'll just call Ravinder!! He will come and deal with you.

(She goes to the telephone and dials the shop. Mrs Arora comes after her, and presses the speaker button, so she can hear everything. The wall clock shows the time to be exactly four forty.)

Poonam: Hullo, Ravinder.

Ravinder: (his surprised voice comes over the speaker) Yes, Mummy. What's been happening? Is everything all right? Why are you calling so early? There is still half an hour to go for the celebrations, you know.

Poonam: **Ravinder!!** (breaks down on hearing his voice) I'm not Mummyji speaking. I'm Poonam, damn it! (starts sobbing)

Ravinder: (startled) Poonam? What happened? Where are you calling from?

Poonam: I'm calling from the house. Please come home immediately, Ravinder.

Ravinder: Why? What's happened ?

Poonam: (bawling now) You know what . . . Mummyji has tried to . . . (breaks down). Just come home, Ravinder. Immediately.

Ravinder: All right, all right, 1'm just coming (addressing Papaji, who's apparently sitting close-by in the shop) No, Papaji, it's nothing to worry. You stay at the shop only, but cancel the celebrations, (addresses Poonam) I'm just coming over. I'll be there in two minutes.

(Poonam puts down the receiver in a tearful exhaustion)

Mrs Arora: (hands on her hips, trying to intimidate a hysterical Poonam) You dirty bitch.

Poonam: (not to be cowed down anymore) You're a witch. An evil witch, if ever there was one. Just wait till Ravinder gets home. He'll tell you how to behave with me.

Mrs Arora: Yes, let my son come back. I'll have you thrashed, bitch. My son will beat you black and blue.

Poonam: Don't you threaten me you thin witch.

Mrs Arora: You fat cow!

Poonam: Witch!

Mrs Arora: Cow!

Poonam: Witch!

Mrs Arora: Oh, I don't have to wait for Ravinder. I'll get rid of you myself, you slut!

(She goes into the kitchen and comes out with a butcher's knife.)

Poonam: Don't come close to me, you mad woman !

(Mrs Arora makes a lunge in Poonam's direction, the carving knife in her hands.)

Mrs Arora: Here. take this, slut!

(Poonam deftly steps aside.)

Mrs Arora: (bounces off the wall. is rattled) Where did she go? (turns to see a frightened looking Poonam) Oh, there you are! You can't escape me!

(She prepares to make another lunge. Meanwhile Poonam has adopted a martial arts pose.)

Mrs Arora: (makes a lunge) Here, take this, you bitch!

Poonam: (gives off a flying kick, taekwondo style) And you take this, you witch!

(Mrs Arora falls to the floor, looking quite dazed. The knife falls with a rattling noise on to the floor. It's her turn now to look frightened.)

Enter Ravinder

Ravinder: Hullo, what's happening here?

Poonam: (rashes towards Ravinder, sobbing) Ravinder, Ravinder .....

Ravinder: Stand aside, woman. What have you done to my mother?

Mrs Arora: Ravinder *beta,* it's good you have come . . ..

Ravinder: I knew I shouldn't have gone, mother. I went against my better judgement. Anyhow, now that I'm here we can put an end to all these problems. Right, mother?

Mrs Arora: Yes, *beta*. Now that she knows everything, we have to get rid off her anyhow.

(Ravinder moves threateningly towards Poonam. She adopts a martial arts pose and gives him a kick in the chest as he advances towards her. A bewildered Ravinder falls to the ground, gets up and advances towards her again. She hands him another taekwondo kick, in the face this time. He gets up determinedly, and with greater aggression this time.)

Ravinder: (advances aggressively) Do you think you can hold me off, you whore?

Mrs Arora: That's the way, my son. Kill the bitch.

Poonam: (scared now) Don't come close to me, I tell you don't come close to me.

(Poonam tries to kick once more, but Ravinder deflects it this time, grabs hold of her hair and pulls her down to his knees. He then kicks her to the ground, and puts his foot on a sobbing Poonam's stomach).

Ravinder: Mother, can you please get me the match-box from the kitchen.

Mrs Arora: (fairly recovered, and visibly cheerful now) At once, my dear.

(Mrs Arora goes into the kitchen to fetch the match box. She finds it next to the newly installed kerosene stove on the kitchen table, comes out and gives it to Ravinder)

Ravinder: (strikes a match) Damn, these matches are damp.

Mrs Arora: They are just fine, son. Here, give them to me....

Poonam: (struggling) Help! Help!! Is there anyone? Help!!

(Just then the police party accompanied by Mrs Bajaj, Madhu and Gulshan arrive at the door).

Policeman: (loudly) Open up in the name of the law!

Ravinder: Who is it?

Policeman: (loudly) Police!!

(When he hesitates, they break open the door)

Scene 10

(On seeing the police party enter. Ravinder releases Poonam Mrs Arora starts cowering in a corner.)

Enter

Inspector Zile Singh, Lawyer Madhu, Mrs Bajaj, Gulshan and Three Constables

Poonam: (sobbing) Oh, *didi.* Mummy, Gulshan *bhaiya.* I'm so happy to see you. (crashes into Gulshan's arms)

Gulshan: (stroking her) There, there, my darling sister.

Mrs Arora: (to Ravinder) See. See. I told you, these two are not brother and sister.

Madhu: See, Inspector, it's just as I feared. There is the can of kerosene in the corner. We seem to have caught them in flagrant delicto.

Inspector: (softly) That's right madam, although please spare me these legal expressions, Let me handle this. (loudly) Hullo, hullo. What do we have here? A can of kerosene, a match-box (picks up the match-box which has fallen to the floor) and a young lady doused with kerosene. Do we need any more proof? Constables, arrest this man and that old woman.

(Two constables go to Ravinder and slip handcuffs on to him. A third female constable goes to Mrs Arora.)

Ravinder: (blustering) Do you know who I am?

Inspector: I've seen many young puppies like you. You obviously haven't heard of me. *Arre,* Inspector Zile Singh hasn't even spared the kids of the Chief Minister of this State. Who the hell are you?

Mrs Arora: There has been a terrible mistake, Inspector. I can explain everything.

Inspector: Go ahead, madam, I'm listening.

Mrs Arora: (points at Poonam) This girl here was trying to set me on fire with the kerosene, when my son Ravinder luckily happened to come home early and rescued me.

Inspector: (sarcastically) Is that so, madam? Is that why her clothes are drenched with kerosene and not yours?

Mrs Arora: Well, I fought back naturally, and in the struggle, she got splashed with some kerosene.

Inspector: And does that explain why your son had his foot on the young lady's stomach just now when we broke open the door?

Mrs Arora: (the fight has gone out of her) Well, you see.. ..

Inspector: (addressing the constable who is standing next to Mrs Arora) Constable, what are you doing? Why haven't you slapped the handcuffs on the accused?

Constable: Sir, I thought that such an old woman..

Inspector: Don't be fooled by those grey hairs, constable. She looks quite dangerous to me. Just then the bell rings.

Enter Papaji

Inspector: Welcome! Welcome! We have been waiting for you. Unfortunately, as you may have noticed, there has been a slight change in the programme.

Papaji: (in some distress to see the police) (weakly) What is happening here? Why has the police come?

Inspector: Don't try and pretend to be so innocent, mister. This here is a clear conspiracy by you, your wife and son to burn the daughter in law of the house.

Papaji: What utter nonsense !

Inspector: No nonsense, sir. They have been caught red handed. We will soon put some sense into your brain. Constable , put this old man in handcuffs as well.

Poonam: (cries out) No, no, Papaji is innocent. He is the only innocent person..

Inspector: Listen, sister, you don't understand these persons. I know this type very well. They are all in this conspiracy together. Constable, arrest this old fogey.

Papaji: (protesting) But, what is my crime? Let me know that at least.

Inspector: Didn't you here me the first time. Conspiracy to burn daughter in law on account of unfulfilled dowry demands. Section 498A and Section 302 of the Indian Penal Code read with Section 34. Are you satisfied? (in a sneering tone) Have you understood the offence you are being charged with?

Madhu: Inspector *sahab,* thank you very very much.

Mrs Bajaj: You brought us here just in the nick of time, otherwise it would have been too late.

Inspector: No, no, madam, this was my duty. Constables, put the accused into the van and take them to the station house, I will follow in my jeep. One of you can remain here to wait for the police photographer and finger print expert who should be coming in any time.

Madhu: Inspector, do you need us to come to the Station?

Inspector: Yes. I need to record all your statements. I also need you to provide me with a list of dowry items that we can seize from the house. Jewellery, TV set, Refrigerator, whatever.

Madhu: Come, Auntyji. Let's go to the police station and get this over with. We can follow the Inspector's jeep in my Maruti. Will it take long, Inspector *sahab?*

Inspector: (addressing Madhu) Your statement will not take long, madam and we will record it first. We'll need much more time with the girl, but even in her case there is no need to record the full statement today. Don't worry about anything, ladies. You'll all be free in an hours time today. As you know very well, all of you will have to appear as witnesses in the Court.

Madhu: That's right, of course. We will cooperate in every possible way, Inspector. May I know the Judge's name who deals with the dowry demand cases.

Inspector: It's a new judge now. (scratches his head) Someone recently transferred from Banaras.

Madhu: Never mind. Inspector . We'll find out in due course.

Scene 11

(The Public Prosecutor and the Judge are drinking coffee and waiting for the lawyer to arrive. The prosecutor has just finished telling the story)

Prosecutor: So, that's the story, Judge. Now you decide?

Judge: Very interesting, I must say, but it just proves what I was saying right in the beginning about innocent parties.

Prosecutor: Innocent parties? How do you mean?

Judge: Well, take the boy's father, Papaji. He was completely innocent, wasn't he?

Prosecutor: Yes, that's true.

Judge: All the same he gets arrested and implicated in the case.

Prosecutor: Well, he got arrested no doubt, but a while, they will drop charges against him.

Judge: Well, they might but that's because you are there. I'm not so sure this would happen elsewhere. And even if it's only a few weeks, he was completely innocent, wasn't he? Why should an innocent party suffer?

Prosecutor: That's true. Ideally, He should not have been involved at all, but it's difficult to have a completely perfect system, judge.

Judge: It is a pity our defence lawyer wasn't here to hear it. Let's discuss this case further when He is here. It will make the discussion more balanced.

Prosecutor: I suppose you're so used to hearing both sides.

Judge: Yes, that's true. Why don't we play a few rounds of flash in the meanwhile?

Prosecutor: All right. Cut for deal.

(The prosecutor shuffles the pack, and then he and the judge pick out one card each.)

Prosecutor: You have the higher card . Your deal, Judge.

(The Judge deals and wins the first round. A few rounds are played in silence, and each time the Judge takes away some winnings from the table)

Prosecutor: (frustrated) Your luck is really good today Judge.

Judge: (in a satisfied tone) *Yes,* isn't it? I should have bought a lottery ticket today.

(There is the sound of a car's engine running.)

Prosecutor: That's the sound of the lawyer's car

Judge: So he's finally reached.

Prosecutor: (relieved) Yes, we can play some rummy now, instead of flash.

Enter The Lawyer

Prosecutor: Late again, Mr Lawyer. You are lucky it wasn't Your Honour's Court.

Judge: (laughing) That's true. His case would certainly have been dismissed in default by now.

Lawyer: A thousand apologies. Your Honour .

Prosecutor: No excuses. We've decided to impose costs on you.

Lawyer: Ah ha ! And what will these be?

Prosecutor: You pay for the refreshments for today and the next five occasions.

Judge: (hastily) Wait a minute, Mr Prosecutor. I don't think we should go so far.

Prosecutor: No, Judge. We shouldn't let him off the hook this time. I mean this is the second time he's late. This is an insult to us.

Judge: But let's at least give him a chance. Perhaps there is an explanation, a justifiable cause for being late.

Lawyer: There is, Your Honour, there is. In truth I had to finalise a Habeas Corpus petition and have it filed so that it can come up before the Division Bench first thing tomorrow morning.

Judge: (soberly) Oh, I see. Well, that's very important undoubtedly. Someone's liberty is at stake.

Lawyer: Exactly, Your Honour. As private counsel, I don't have the liberties permitted to my friend here.

Prosecutor: Such as?

Lawyer: Taking it easy. You're assured of your monthly wages, aren't you? No matter how hard you work. Or don't.

Prosecutor: Why don't you pick and choose a few cases here and there? That way you'll be able to keep your appointments (taunting) Or aren't you in that position as yet?

Lawyer: I'm certainly in a better position than some people I know.

Prosecutor: What are you implying?

Lawyer: Everyone knows how it's only the failed lawyers who decide to become Prosecutors. A prosecutor's earnings don't exactly measure up to a privy purse, do they?

Prosecutor: Are you saying that your Honour here is also a failed lawyer?

Lawyer: Did I ever say that?

Prosecutor: Well, you imply that. There's not much difference between what a prosecutor earns and a judge earns at the District Court level, so what you say about me will apply to judges as well. And are you boasting about how much you earn?

Lawyer: You son of a.... You're putting words into my mouth, (anxious). Your Honour, I never said that! Being, a judge is something entirely different.

Prosecutor: I seem to remember someone gave an examination two years ago to be appointed as a Public Prosecutor, and couldn't pass.

Lawyer: Oh, that! I wasn't serious!! It was to win a bet.

Prosecutor: What was the bet? You'd succeed in failing the exam. That's wasn't so difficult for you.

Lawyer: Don't be so jealous my friend. If you had only stuck to private practice, you'd have made it too. And have had your clients buying you plane tickets for Court appearances in other States.

Prosecutor: (in a sneering tone). So, for this case you'll be catching the early morning flight to Allahabad early tomorrow morning, I suppose. It's coming up before the Allahabad High Court, isn't it?

Lawyer: No, it's coming up before the Delhi High Court as a matter of fact.

Prosecutor: (pauses, then says dramatically) This is his standard excuse. Your Honour, (mimicking the lawyer). I was busy preparing a Habeas Corpus petition for the High Court. . . and our District Court judges here are all so completely taken in. . . and are extremely indulgent to our friend here.

Lawyer: (angrily) Don't *make* false accusations, Mr Lawyer.

Prosecutor: (addressing the judge, in an innocent voice) Who is accusing anyone? I was just making an observation that our friend here is such a big shot district lawyer that clients engage him for the High Court at Allahabad -and the Delhi High Court as well, I learn now-ignoring the thousands of lawyers regularly practising there.

Lawyer: He is just jealous of my success, that's it, Judge.

Prosecutor: (angrily) I'm not jealous!! How dare you make such statements. I challenge you to tell us the names of the High Court judges before whom the petition is coming up tomorrow morning.

Lawyer: I refuse to divulge confidential details to such a . . .

Judge: Calm down, calm down gentlemen. This is not a Court of Law. (amused at his own joke) You are both unnecessarily getting excited.

Prosecutor: (in an easy tone) Don't worry, Judge. We always talk to each other like this. It doesn't mean anything.

Judge: We were supposed to be having a relaxed game of rummy. At least I hope we are going to start now. You know Mr Lawyer, Mr Public Prosecutor was only just now telling *me* about a most interesting case of one Poonam from Delhi.

Lawyer: Oh. that Model Town case involving the Bajaj family and the Arora family.

Judge: (startled) That's right, Mr Lawyer. I'm surprised you know about it.

Lawyer: (proudly) Oh, I know all about that case. Some relative of the Arora family came to my office yesterday to engage me on their behalf. They are all still in jail as you know.

Prosecutor: I must say you keep the most efficient and hard working touts, Mr lawyer.

Judge: Take it easy, Mr Prosecutor. Don't let's start again. Why do you wish to trouble our friend? Come on, let's have each person's opinion on this case. Why don't you begin by telling us your views, Mr Lawyer, since you are going to be handling this case on behalf of the Arora family?

Prosecutor: The judge was commenting on how the father in law, a completely innocent party was falsely implicated.

Lawyer: Yes, that's of course a completely black and white situation. Why, the man is practically a saint. Everybody says so in Princes Bazaar. I should be able to get him out on bail in two, three days.

Prosecutor: Well, at least you accept that as far as the rest of the family was concerned, I mean Ravinder and Mrs Arora, justice was done.

Lawyer: I'm not so sure.

Prosecutor: How do you mean, Mr lawyer. This is an open and shut case.

Lawyer: Yes, but there were aggravating circumstances.

Prosecutor: Aggravating circumstances for attempted murder. I don't understand what you mean.

Lawyer: Well, take the conduct of this girl Poonam for instance.

Prosecutor: What about her conduct? Nothing wrong with it.

Lawyer: You have to admit that dowry apart, there were other reasons for the mother-in-law to be upset with her.

Prosecutor: What other reasons?

Lawyer: Well obviously she was not a woman of good character. The mother-in-law's suspicions about her were entirely justified.

Prosecutor: That's no excuse for murder.

Judge: Let's hear Mr Lawyer out fully, Mr Prosecutor. He is entitled to express his views.

Lawyer: Thank you, Judge. Well, as I said one thing I did not like on the part of the Bajaj family was how they deceived the Arora's into thinking that the Model Town house was theirs, and that they even owned a factory. Secondly, Judge . . . frankly, I don't know what is happening to girls nowadays. They are turning more and more like men. Take this girl Poonam now. Why should a girl want to learn martial arts and try to be like a man? It's most improper.

Prosecutor: What nonsense! A girl must learn how to defend herself. There is nothing wrong with that. After all, it was only her expertise in martial arts that saved her in the end. Isn't that right, Judge?

Lawyer: (snidely) Martial arts is not the only thing she learnt from that fellow Gulshan. That's my third point.

Prosecutor: How can you make such insinuations, Mr Lawyer about a perfectly innocuous and platonic brother-sister relationship! And none of your arguments would carry any weight in a Court of Law.

Lawyer: It appears that you don't know the real meaning of the word 'platonic' Mr Prosecutor, (pauses). It means play for him and tonic for her.

(All three off them have a good laugh over this, the Public Prosecutor loudest of all.)

Lawyer: (resuming) Platonic, my foot. This girl Poonam has been getting fucked regularly by this fellow Gulshan for several years now. Ask anyone in Model Town, Delhi, It's an open secret...

Prosecutor: Language, Mr Lawyer, language. You are not sitting in your chamber drinking beer with your gangster clients. This is a public place and you are in esteemed company.

Judge: Seriously, Mr Lawyer, if that was the case that these two were having a relationship what stopped them from getting married.

Lawyer: No, no, that was not possible, Judge.

Prosecutor: (interested) The Judge has made a valid point. Mr Lawyer. Why couldn't they have got married?

Lawyer: Very simple. This fellow Gulshan did not have a sufficiently high status. The Bajaj family wanted to get a decent boy from a high status family, and Gulshan and Poonam thought they could carry on with their relationship in Ghaziabad.

Prosecutor: Now you are talking bull shit, Mr lawyer, excuse my saying so.

Judge: No, no, the defence lawyer has made a plausible case. Since we are on the subject, leaving aside the question of the guilt of the Arora's for the time being, let me say that it is my firm belief that no well-bred girl from a decent family could have such a sexual appetite such that I have heard from the prosecutor.

Prosecutor: Come off it, Judge. Women too have the same sexual appetites as men.

Judge: With respect, Mr Prosecutor, there I must. disagree with you. You see, here lies the difference between a girl from a cultured, decent family and a *bazaaru* type of girl. The second type of girl can only think of sex. (in a challenging tone). Let me ask you about your wife, Mr Prosecutor. You tell me, what kind of lady is she?

Lawyer: (laughing) Mr Prosecutor did not marry, judge so he cannot answer your question, but I think you are absolutely right. You have hit the nail on the head. It wasn't the Arora family's fault that they got such a *chaalu* girl.

Judge: I have to agree with you, Mr Lawyer. Mr Prosecutor, what do you think?

Prosecutor: Quite frankly I don't understand what you and Mr Lawyer are talking about.

Judge: Well surely you must admit that the dowry was not the only reason why an attempt was made on *the* girl's life.

Prosecutor: As I said before, I don't understand. What other reason was there?

Lawyer: Come now, Mr Prosecutor, you have to admit that you haven't told the true story, have you? And Your Honour here has been clever enough to catch you out.

Prosecutor: Mr Lawyer, I tell you I have spoken the truth! I'm serious now. I'm not Joking

Judge: The truth as you would like to believe it-as a Prosecutor.

Lawyer: Exactly!

Prosecutor: It's the truth, judge.

Lawyer: Tell me, Judge, did the prosecutor make out the motive for this case-attempted murder admittedly-to be based entirely on dowry demands.

Prosecutor: More or less. More or less .

Lawyer: And he did not speak about this girl's character at all.

Judge: No, to be fair to him he did disclose the facts, but he chose not to draw the most logical and obvious inferences.

Prosecutor: Which were?

Judge: Firstly, that this Poonam was a woman of loose morals.

Prosecutor: How did you deduce that, Judge?

Judge: It's perfectly obvious. Her amazing sexual expertise and appetite. Less than two weeks after her marriage, she is teaching her husband sexual positions. That suggests a great deal of experience.

Prosecutor: Not necessarily, judge. Maybe she read them in a textbook.

Judge: It shows you what kind of stuff she was reading then. Nice girls don't read *Kama Sutra*.

Prosecutor: Look, judge, I don't agree with you-but assuming for a moment that I did accept that the girl had sexual experience before her marriage, what difference would that make?

Judge: From a purely legal point of view, I grant you that it would have made no difference. The Court cannot consider the girl's past character to be relevant in such cases. The Supreme Court has held so in a number of decisions. However from a moral point of view...

Prosecutor: (interrupting) I don't see how any of this is relevant from a moral point of view either.

Lawyer: Come now, Mr Prosecutor. Don't let the jadge think that you are as depraved as all that. Would you accept that this girl Poonam had a bad reputation, or to be more accurate, had no reputation to speak of at all?

Prosecutor: I don't know that. This is news to me, Mr Lawyer.

Lawyer: Well, let me tell you, since I'm dealing with this case now, I've had some background checks done on this girl, and I tell you that they confirm that the girl had a very ill-reputation.

Judge: That does not surprise me at all.

Lawyer: Lies ! All lies!!

Judge: Mr Prosecutor, you will admit that the story you told me was derived from what this girl Poonam told you.

Prosecutor: Yes. I do accept that.

Judge: So it's the girl's version of events, isn't it?

Prosecutor: Well, yes.

Judge: And how do you know that the girl's version is the truth?

Prosecutor: It's the truth, judge. I've talked to the girl myself. I've cross-examined hundreds of complainants. I can make out when a person is telling lies.

Judge: I'm not saying she only spoke lies. However undoubtedly she concealed certain facts.

Prosecutor: So what then, according to you, is the real truth?

Judge: Mr Defence Lawyer?

Lawyer: Yes, Judge.

Judge: Will you tell us if there is another version of events?

Lawyer: Most certainly there is, Your Honour. I have had two lengthy interviews with the accused persons who are still in prison. Mr Arora of course knew nothing at all, being completely innocent in the entire affair, so there wasn't any point even in questioning him. However I have spoken at length with Mrs Arora and the boy Ravinder, and ascertained the true facts of the case.

Judge: Interesting. And what were these facts? Mr Prosecutor, I hope you are listening.

Lawyer: As I understand it, the boy Ravinder was quite happy with the girl in the beginning, even though there was not much dowry, and they had been quite simply cheated and deceived by the girl's family. He changed his mind about the girl however when his mother disclosed to him the real facts regarding the girl's relationship with Gulshan.

Prosecutor: They were like brother and sister.

Lawyer: There is a part in this story that you know nothing about, Mr Prosecutor, because the girl could not have told you about it. There was an incident when the brother Gulshan was supposed to have removed a speck of dust from Poonam's eyes; did she mention that to you?

Prosecutor: Yes, of course, and I have informed the judge about that incident.

Lawyer: Ah, but the truth is that on that occasion something else transpired. When Gulshan came to visit Poonam a second time the two lovers had been separated for far too long for them to be able to control themselves. They fell upon each other with great fervour and passion as soon as the mother in law had withdrawn. Confident that the mother in law lay asleep in the Bedroom they lay down on the drawing room carpet, the girl on top of the boy kissing, hugging and caressing each other for a full fifteen minutes. Then, their passion satiated somewhat, they suddenly realised that the mother in law might wake up, and went back to sit on the sofa. Mrs Arora had actually gone to the bathroom to clean the toilet bowl, when the sounds of their lovemaking alerted her, and keeping the bathroom door ajar slightly, she watched stealthily for the full fifteen minutes. She was too shocked to react immediately. It was only when the two lovers were seated on the sofa exchanging a last lingering kiss that she strode in. As far as the two were concerned however, they were confident that Mrs Arora had actually not witnessed anything beyond that fellow Gulshan leaning over Poonam, and the eye speck business was quickly invented as an excuse for the curious posture in which she found them.

Prosecutor: If this was the case, why did Ravinder go to the girl's house to get her back? That's not the behaviour of a husband who realises he has been cuckolded.

Lawyer: Oh, that's because Mrs Arora didn't tell him anything till they came back. She had been holding herself back, not wanting to break up the son's marriage. At length, she decided she had to tell him, and they had to get rid of the girl to protect the honour of the family.

Prosecutor: Come now, Mr Lawyer, these are common tactics used by defence counsel in rape cases. The standard ploy used there is to besmirch the reputation of the girl. You produce false witnesses and make it out to be a case where the raped girl is seen to be practically doing night shifts in the red light area.. and you'll succeed in getting the rapist off the hook.

Lawyer: This is not a rape case!

Prosecutor: Exactly!! So all these ploys don't make any sense to me. It will not convince anyone.

Lawyer: We are discussing matters from an extra legal point of view as the Judge said. My arguments are convincing Your Honour.

Prosecutor: No, they aren't.

Judge: Listen to me, both of you. I know of a case just like this one that took place in Banaras some years ago.

Lawyer: Ah ha. Yes, judge. Precedent always helps us in realising the truth.

Judge: Very similar case. The mother-in-law was dissatisfied with the dowry. Much more so than the boy.

Prosecutor: How can you know that for certain, Judge? I know that boys these days wait for dowry items more eagerly than his parents. Affer all if it is a Maruti 1000 or an Esteem, it is the boy who will be driving it. Before the marriage, they fantasize about the possibility of getting this brand new car at the time of the wedding-and when they don't get it, the hopes which they have built up during the waiting period are dashed to the ground. They are furious with the girl and her family and then the whole dowry extraction game begins.

Judge: In this case the boy was not interested in dowry at all.

Prosecutor: Are you sure, Judge?

Judge: Yes, I'm very sure.

Prosecutor: We'll take your word on it then.

Judge: I knew the boy very well.

(The Public Prosecutor's ears prick up. He leans close to the table, eagerly listening now)

Prosecutor: Yes, Judge?

Judge: I grant you the mother was fairly disappointed in the girl as well as the dowry, as in this case.

Prosecutor: Yes, Judge, go on.

Lawyer: I'm glad to see you listening so patiently, Mr Prosecutor.

Judge: (continues) The girl was a corrupt one. On the wedding night itself-what they call the *suhag raat,* where the girl is expected to be pure, virginal-she wanted more and more.

Prosecutor: Nothing wrong with that.

Judge: Well... that was not all.

Prosecutor: So then tell us judge. What was'all' ? Don't be shy. We're all friends here.

Judge: (hesitating) Well, she wanted to...

Prosecutor: Was it fellatio, judge, she wanted to?

Judge: Yes.

Prosecutor: And was that all?

Judge: No, she wanted the other thing as well.

Prosecutor: You mean cunnilingus.

Judge: Exactly

Lawyer: Mr Prosecutor is an expert with all this terminology. I tell you, he is a regular with the ladies at *bhindi* bazaar.

Prosecutor: (ignoring the lawyer) So what does all this mean, Judge?

Judge: You know very well what it means, Mr Prosecutor. The boy was shocked, traumatized even. The nice, decent girl he was expecting turned out to be someone entirely different. However he still wanted to continue with the marriage, but one day something happened.

Prosecutor: Yes?

Judge: He came home early from the Courts.

Prosecutor: Was he a lawyer, Judge?

Judge: (hesitates slightly) Yes, yes. He came home early from the Courts and he found the girl had been sent packing to her parent's house.

Prosecutor: And why was that done?

Judge: Similar story to the present one. The girl too had a lover, a so-called brother-someone of lower status, whom the family couldn't consider her getting married to.

Prosecutor: And he came to her house?

Judge: That's right.

Prosecutor: And the boy's mother caught them in the act.

Judge: Just like Gulshan and Poonam were caught. Now you're admitting it, Mr Prosecutor. I knew it when you were first telling the story that the eye speck business was just a made up tale. Who would believe it?

Prosecutor: It was not made up, Judge.

Judge: It was, Mr Prosecutor, it was. The facts are too similar.

Prosecutor: How are you certain that the boy's mother was not lying?

Judge: Well, it tied in, didn't it?

Prosecutor: With what?

Judge: With her advanced knowledge and experience of sexual matters.

Prosecutor: There is another rather obvious possibility, isn't there judge?

Judge: Another possibility What do you mean?

Prosecutor: Don't tell me it didn't occur to you. It's entirely possible, don't you think, that the mother in law had decided to get rid of the daughter-in-law and invented a tale, which she knew would sound plausible to the son.

Judge: (in confusion) No, no, that's not possible, (angrily) I'm telling you, it's not possible. (shouts) The girl was a .. slut.

Lawyer: Why are you annoying the judge, Mr Prosecutor? What pleasure do you derive?

Prosecutor: Don't interrupt us, Mr Lawyer, (turns to the judge) And what happened next?

Judge: (recovering himself) Well, as in this case, the girl came back two days later, shamefaced at having been caught in flagrant delicto-isn't that the expression? - but pretending as if nothing had happened.

Prosecutor: And then?

Judge: The boy accepted the mother's suggestion that they plan out a kitchen accident. The difference was...

Lawyer: Yes?!!

Prosecutor: Yes?!

Judge: (quietly) It worked!!

(There is a silence)

Prosecutor: That was murder!

Lawyer: Aggravating circumstances.

Judge: I' m quite sure none of this would have happened, had the girl's character not been fatally blemished,

Prosecutor: So you feel this was justified, Judge?

Judge: No, not perhaps justified, but certainly understandable. Yes. Certainly understandable.

Prosecutor: Were they prosecuted?

Judge: As a matter of fact they never were.

Prosecutor: So they got away with it. And you didn't do anything about it.

Judge: No, I couldn't.

Prosecutor: Couldn't or wouldn't?

Judge: Couldn't.

Prosecutor: It's because you knew the family?

Lawyer: They were relatives, man.

Judge: Yes, I knew them. They were relatives, (musing) How can one know in advance? Let me confess to you, gentlemen, that my first wife too was such a girl as this Poonam.

Prosecutor: (eyes popping out) Really, Judge? In which respect ?

Judge: Well, you know . . . she thought of sex all the time. All the time. She drove me crazy. Now. . . my wife at present, whom I married after the first one's death is a perfect lady.

Prosecutor: So sorry to hear about the death of your wife, Judge.

Judge: It was all for the better , I think .As I was saying, there were problems there. I have been much happier with my present wife.

Prosecutor: I'm sure she lies in bed like a corpse while Your Honour is banging away at her.

Judge: (angrily) Mr Prosecutor!!

Prosecutor: You've been winning all the games so far. Judge. I'm entitled to a little fun as well.

Judge: (still angry) I didn ' t say anything about your wife !!

Prosecutor: I don't have a wife, Judge didn't you hear the defence lawyer-so you could say anything you liked about her. (sees the Judge's expression) Sorry, Judge, I was just joking.

Lawyer: Don't mind him, Judge. Mr Prosecutor is a totally debauch and can't help talking like this. You see, he visits prostitutes every night. That's where he picks up his colourful expressions from. I wouldn't be at all surprised if that's where he's headed after our rummy game is over.

Prosecutor: I've seen you there myself more than once, Mr Lawyer, so don't try and get all virtuous with me. And you a married fellow with no excuse for it, unlike poor lonesome me. And when I do go to see them, at least I pay for their services, (sniggers) I'm told you adjust it with your fees for defending the ladies. It is my guess that that's what delayed you while coming here. All this habeas corpus stuff is just some lies you invented on the way.

Lawyer: (apoplectic) Mr Prosecutor . . .(shouting) I warn you!!

Judge: Gentlemen, please! You are squabbling again.

(The two lawyers fall silent, glaring angrily at each other. After a minute, they break into a subdued laughter. The defence lawyer then picks up the deck of cards, shuffles them and deals them out.)

Lawyer: By the way, Judge, how did your first wife die?

Judge: (visibly embarrassed) Well . . you see . . . there was . . .

Prosecutor: (murmurs) A small accident in the kitchen perhaps.

Judge: (serious now) Pick up your cards, Mr Prosecutor

Prosecutor: Like your so-called relative.

Judge: I said . . .

Prosecutor: Your Honour?

Judge: (with anger) Pick up your cards, Mr Prosecutor.

CONQUEST AT NOON

A Historical Fantasy

A fantasy play on the theme of colonialism / racism

Dedication
for
Sagari

List Of Characters

General Brandy the Commander of the Bharatian Army during the reign of Jahanpanah. He is also in his second role simply GENERAL, the director of the play 'CONQUEST AT NOON'.

Princess Ujala, direct descendant of the Limshumdin Emperor Karan Karim, Queen Empress of Maha Bharat. She is also in her second role, simply PRINCESS, an actress in the play 'CONQUEST AT NOON.'

Prince Chanakaya, a suitor for the hand of Princess Ujala. In his second role, he is simply CHANAKAYA an actor in the play.

Prince Socrates, another suitor for the hand of Princess Ujala, he is the Prince of an unconquered island near Blighty. He is also simply SOCRATES, a white actor from an island near Blighty chosen for the role of Prince Socrates.

Jahanpanah (or J.P. for short), the Princess's great-grandfather, who ruled the Bharatian Empire and presided over its most repressive phase.

Sanjay, the Princess's great-uncle and teacher, who provides her with a clear view of the past. He also plays the role of SUTRADHAAR in the play 'CONQUEST AT NOON'.

General Brandy, J.P.'s commander-in-chief, who is responsible for the awful sterilization episode near the city of Tundun.

Colonel Mossambi, his right hand man

Birchbill, revolutionary leader of Blighty

Clementine, his wife

Behru, the Bharatian Prime Minister, during the reign of J.P.

Devtee Lion, a young, militant revolutionary from Blighty

Sunpearl Lion, his aristocratic father, a prominent lawyer in Blighty

Lady Mohabattein, a friend and confidante of Clementine

Col Chaudhury, the Commander of the Bharatian Army during the reign of Princess Ujala

Mr Gundu, Defense Minister during the reign of Princess Ujala

Mr Dang, a Senior Cabinet Minister during the reign of Princess Ujala

Mr Shobhraj, a Senior Cabinet Minister during the reign of Princess Ujala

Guruji, Head Priest and important religious leader during the reign of Princess Ujala

Shabdgamini, a learned linguist with five doctorates who can speak all the twenty-seven languages spoken in Maha Bharat.

Khidmatdar, a servant in the palace

Three soldiers, a Secretary, a maid-in -waiting, two footmen, a doorman, a doctor, a nurse, and a group of protestors

List Of Dates

1556 - 1605 AD (anno domini): According to the system of dates followed in Blighty, this period coincides with the period of the reign of the Great Emperor Karan Karim, when two great world religions were consolidated with the coming of the great mystic Sant Kabir, which led to the consolidation of territory in the sub-continent and the establishment of Maha Bharat.

1605 - 1856 AD: A period of tremendous scientific and industrial progress in Maha Bharat contemporaneous with the conquest of a great deal of overseas territory, the subjugation of the island of Blighty being particularly notable, (described by later historians as the 'jewel in the crown' of the Bhartian Empire) as it set the seal on further conquests of later Bhartian Emperors.

1857 AD : There is mutiny in Blighty. The Blitz, the Bots and the Welshy come together in a valiant attempt to throw out the foreign power. The Virish people on a neighboring island however come to the rescue of the Bharatian army and with their support the rebellion is crushed. The putting down of the rebellion is accompanied by the siege and destruction of the city of Tundun. There is tremendous slaughter, arson and looting of the treasures of that ancient city.

1930 -1945 AD : A period of time when the Bhartian Empire rapidly disintegrates, losing several of its most prized possessions including the territory of Blighty. The Emperor at this point of history is, as stated earlier, Jahanpanah, Princess U's great-grandfather. The Blitz independence movement is led mainly by moderate leaders Birchbill and Sunpearl Lion. There are militant factions who also participate and lend energy to the movement and the killing of Devtee Lion, militant leader of the Blitz Krieg sparks countrywide protests.

1947: The *swayamvara* of Princess Ujala is held. It has global consequences and the world will never be the same again.

(Note: Dates are given above mainly according to the Blitz calendar. The reader must not forget that prior to rapid development and cultural progress, which accelerated during the reign of Emperor Karan Karim, there was not much difference between the Bharatian civilization and civilization in Blighty. The Blitz too had a moderately developed culture in some respects (though colonizers would argue that it was visibly inferior, even at that time) and there is no denying the fact that they were the first to give the world the idea of history and dates. Their calendar is therefore still in vogue, though some Bharatian ultra-nationalists prefer to use the Bharatian calendar which came into being on the demise of the Great Emperor, Karan Karim. Interested readers can make the necessary adjustment if need be. Suffice it to say, that as is well known, we are currently in the year 2010A.D. according to the Blitz calendar, whereas as per the Bharatian calendar we are in 405 A.K.K.)

Scene 1

The scene opens on to a large, well furnished office. There is a white haired, casually dressed gentleman sitting behind a desk. He has a slightly mad, creative air about him. All along the walls of the room are hung framed stills from various theatre productions.

Enter A Secretary

Secretary : There is a gentleman here who wishes to see you. Shall I ask him to wait?

General : What does he look like?

Secretary : He's tall, has long hair and a beard . . . and he's white.

General : That must be Socrates. Send him in at once. And oh, Sevanti, will you send in two cups of strongly brewed tea?

Secretary : Yes, sir. And I'm sending the gentleman in.

Exit Secretary

Enter Socrates. He is bearded with long hair, but is dressed formally in a suit with tie.

General : Come in, come in Mr Socrates. Have a seat.

Socrates : Thank you.

General : Yes, what can I do for you? There was something you wanted to talk to me about, wasn't there? I remember your mentioning it at the last rehearsal.

Socrates : (blurts out) It's about money.

General : (raises his eyebrows) You're not happy with

the stipend we're giving you for the production?

Socrates : (protests vehemently) Oh, no, that's not it. That's not it at all. I mean to say, that what you're giving is very handsome. (hesitates)

General : Come out with it, man. Come out with it.

Socrates : The thing is that I want to settle down.

General : I see. Who's the lucky lady, may one ask?

Chanakaya : (hastily) Nobody you know, sir.

General : Is the young lady agreeable?

Socrates : I don't know her views on the subject.

General : (is a surprised tone) What?!

Socrates : (explaining) Because even if she said yes, I wouldn't know how to support her.

General : (is thoughtful) Is she Bharatian?

Socrates : That's right. Had she been Blitz, there wouldn't have been a problem, but seeing as she's Bharatian, she's used to a certain level of comfort.

General : You want to know if there are any long term financial possibilities for you with the company? (shakes his head) No, I'm afraid not. As you know our practice here is that we don't keep actors on a salary. If you keep them on a regular wage, then you do certainly provide them with some security, which young actors badly require, but the downside of this is that you cannot then give new talent a chance thereafter. Say, for instance, if I had full time employed actors in my production company, I would need to give them the parts of Chanakaya and Socrates. I couldn't have taken fresh faces. And now all three of you, you, Chanakaya, and the Princess – you're all three completely fresh faces who haven't ever starred in a big theatre production before.

Socrates : You're right. I understand.

General : What's the problem? She'll wait for you, won't she?

Socrates : I'm not quite sure of that.

General : Well, if she's worth it she will. What do you think?

Socrates : Not necessarily, sir. If she's worth it, someone else with a bigger purse will propose and pick her up soon enough.

General : Pick her up? As if she was a commodity. I'm afraid I don't agree with you. I would sincerely advise you to first propose to the young lady and see her reaction. If she's not willing to wait, forget all about it. Girls will come and go. Concentrate on your performance, my dear. If you manage to win a Fony, you wouldn't need to worry about money at all.

Socrates : I doubt it very much.

General : Don't be pessimistic. You have a great future, Socrates. Dc you know the reason why I gave you the part of Socrates to play?

Socrates : No, sir.

General : It wasn't because you are a brilliant actor.

Socrates : No, sir?

General : I could have had any number of seasoned, mature actors who would have given their eye teeth to get such a role. No. And it wasn't because of the fact that you're white, though I grant you it may have been a part of the reason. For the sake of authenticity. But it was a very small part of the reason, mind you. It also wasn't because I like white people in general, and want to help them out if I can. No, I wouldn't give anyone a role because I was feeling sorry for them. I'd be out of business in six weeks if I did that.

Socrates : (sounds mystified) Why did you take me on then sir? I don't understand.

General : It was because of your responses to my questions *before* the audition for the part. I found your responses to be very mature, very wise and very well articulated. If I may ask how long have you been in Maha Bharat?

Socrates : Nearly two years now, General.

General : Well, I must commend you on your Prustian in that case. Why, your Prustian is almost perfect.

Socrates : It's as good as yours General if I may say so, and it has nothing to do with my having spent time in Bharat. I'm not the only Blitz who can speak a Bhartian language fluently. There are thousands of Blitz who speak fluent Prustian.

General : Point taken, Socrates. As I was saying, you may or may not be a good actor, we're still to determine that, but you carry this air of wisdom about you and so you fitted the character like a glove. Prince Socrates was wise, wasn't he? Just like his earlier namesake. (pauses) Tell me, what is your view about the script?

Socrates : Why, it's excellent.

General : Hmmm. Tell me something, the Bharatians ruled your island for three hundred years, didn't we? Two hundred and fifty to be more precise? (waves his hand) That depends on how you calculate. Anyhow, that's not important. Two hundred, three hundred, it's all the same. Now you're a highly educated Blitz who's had a good exposure to our life and custom, so much so that now you're even planning to marry a Bharatian girl soon as you get the money to do so. What does someone like you who has seen both sides of the picture think of our culture?

Socrates : Which culture are you now talking of?. Your

society has changed enormously these last few decades.

General : (thoughtfully) That's true. I would argue that in the last fifty years, in fact ever since the world became free, it's been downhill for our people as a whole. Why's that? I'll give you some examples. Take the girls for instance. Our girls were shy and decent. It was simply unthinkable for one of our girls to go to bed with a fellow she was not going to marry.

Socrates : On the other hand General this was not entirely a bad thing. She can now make a more informed choice about the person she's going to marry.

General : Informed choice can easily degenerate into promiscuity.

Socrates : That's the other side of it of course.

General : It was the Blitz who had a reputation for promiscuity. Now we're becoming like you.

Socrates : It's a multicultural world today, isn't it?

General : And then in earlier times the younger generation used to respect their elders a great deal. In my youth we used to practically revere our elders.

Socrates : Personally I think it's good that's changing as well. The children from your times were far too controlled. A repressed lot.

General : (amused)What do you know about the childhood of people of my generation, Socrates. Do you see how children here treat their elders now? Like disposable waste.

Socrates : Some elderly people are abused, it is true. I have seen it happening. This was one of the very attractive aspects of your culture undoubtedly – only I wonder if it occasionally went too far. That is all I meant to say.

General : I accept it went too far. You see, Socrates, we

are in agreement on many issues. I miss what I could call 'the good old days.' You see, now even our traditions are no longer what they used to be. Take the arranged marriage system or its more regal variation, the *swayamvara*. Tomorrow we stage our play about Princess Ujala's historic *swayamvara*, don't we? Who holds *swayamvara*'s anymore?!

Socrates : It's quite good actually that *swayamvaras* are not held anymore. In this day and age they are simply not practical anymore.

General : And our system of arranged marriages? What do you think of them?

Socrates : It's a fine system just so long as no one is forced to marry against his choice.

General : Of course they shouldn't. Such abuses did indeed take place earlier. For this reason, I was never convinced that the arranged marriage system was so very superior, or that your system of unregulated free choice was so bad really, as it was made out to be by early colonizers. People of my father's generation did believe strongly that that the white people were barbaric, uncivilized, even savage, and that you desperately needed to have a civilized process for partner selection. I was never fully convinced by these arguments.

Socrates : My father was a great critic of society in Blighty and a firm believer in the values of your society. He was in those days, what was called a white *sahab*. Or a boiled egg. White from the outside and yellow or brown inside. Till the end of his days, he believed that it was cultural attributes such as the free system of partner selection that became the cause of our undoing and defeat.

General : What on earth do arranged marriages have to do with military conquest, Socrates?

Socrates : Don't you see the argument, General? The thesis was that it was precisely because of these cultural attributes– arranged marriages, reverence for elders, strong family ties – that you were a cohesive, integrated society. You became a strong united nation and went ahead and conquered the rest of the world.

General : And your view of this argument is . . .

Socrates : It is persuasive of course...

Enter Secretary

Secretary : The Chairman of the Royal Theatre Company has come to see you.

General : I thought I'd made it clear to him that I will not do another production for the government. Not after they chopped it up so badly the last time. Last time they asked me to stage a production on the Great Emperor Karan Karim and said I would be given complete freedom with the script. Then when they saw the final product, which mind you is based on historical fact, they turned squeamish.

Secretary : What shall I tell him, sir?

General : (grunts) I suppose I'd better see him.

Exit Secretary

Socrates : (standing up) I'd better be getting along.

General : We'll continue this chat some other time. And don't worry so much about the finances. Just concentrate on your work.

Socrates : Thanks for your time.

General : We will meet tomorrow at the theatre two hours before the performance is to begin. Don't be late.

Socrates : Right, General.

Exit Socrates

Scene 2

The scene opens on to a stage whose set has been partially prepared for a luncheon scene. The general décor of the place is grand. It is supposed to represent a large hall in a palace. In the center of this hall, is a staircase running up. The audience can see a large landing next to where this staircase ends. From this landing a visitor to the palace would presumably walk ahead to the other (not visible) rooms of the palace. In the hall tables are laid out, complete with dinner plates, jugs containing sparkling sherbet, and other cutlery. Near the tables, placed at a slight elevation is an enormous throne, studded with rubies, diamonds and emeralds. There is a large revolving globe placed on the table near the throne. Next to the throne is a smaller throne (meant for the Princess's great uncle). A beautiful young girl is sitting on the throne, and seated next to her in the smaller throne is a young man in T-shirt and jeans. The man is clean-shaven, with a shaved head, and is wearing earrings.

Chanakaya : So what's the answer, Saloni?

Princess : Don't call me Saloni.

Chanakaya : Why, that's your name, isn't it?

Princess : Not till the play is over, it isn't. Do I call you by your real name, Pushpinder Singh Ahuja?

Chanakaya : No, you don't but you're welcome to. I won't object.

Princess : Listen, I believe in listening to the directors instructions. The General's order is that everyone who is acting in this play should call the other person by his or her stage name.

Chanakaya : I don't get it. Why insist on this?!

Princess : (explaining) The general feels that this helps us in some way to internalize the characters better into our personalities, and this will come through ultimately in the performances.

Chanakaya : Right. I'll rephrase the question. What is your answer, princess?

Princess : I have told you already Chanakaya, my feelings are engaged elsewhere.

Chanakaya : (jealous) So who's the guy?

Princess : I can't tell you that.

Chanakaya : Is it someone in the play?

Princess : (there is a trace of hesitation in her voice) No, of course not!

Chanakaya : Well, then if you're interested in this other feller, whose name you won't tell me, why don't you marry HIM?

Princess : (quietly) I don't know if he's interested.

Chanakaya : Oh, oh. Well, if he ISN'T interested, then do I have a chance?

Princess : (tearful) What kind of a friend are you, Channi, to wish that I'm turned down by him.

Chanakaya : If you got it that bad, you ought to feel more for me. Seriously sweetheart, I don't want him to turn you down, but we got to consider it's possible.

Princess : (in tears now) It's more than possible. I know it in my bones that he does not care.

Chanakaya : (trying to sound sympathetic) Here, take my handkerchief and wipe your tears. I pray your Prince Charming, whoever he is, says yes, but if it is a no no, give it a thought about hitching your band wagon with me, will ya? Promise me that, Princess.

Princess : (wipes her tears) I suppose so.

Chanakaya : (pressing his advantage / getting bolder) If your guy turns you down and I win the Fony Award for best actor, then you gotta say yes.

Princess : What does winning the Fony award have to do with getting married to anyone, Channi?

Chanakaya : I didn't mean it that way. I know you don't care for money, Princess, but the fact is that a new actor cannot support a family unless and until he gets some big award, and then of course the roles and the money will just start pouring in. Offers from the movie industry as well, you know. There's no limit to the kind of money you can make once you win a Fony.

Princess : (sounding disgusted) Oh, you men are all the same. Always thinking about money. What does marriage have to do with money, I ask you?

Chanakaya : Everything!! Come on girl, you need the money before you can even think about raising a family. It's a big responsibility.

Princess : Marriage is not about velvet sofa sets, carved dining tables and bigger cars. It's not something material.

Chanakaya : What is it then?

Princess : Oh, it's a union of souls. You could live out of a suitcase if you loved each other. (sighs) And what makes you think, Mr Chanakaya, that I wouldn't win the Fony and be a superstar myself. I could easily support a family myself.

Chanakaya : Didn't say you couldn't Princess. My point is that one of them needs to be earning a decent amount. Doesn't matter if it's the woman.

Princess : Channi, what makes you so sure you'll win the Fony for this play. Socrates has an equally powerful role. He could win it instead.

Chanakaya : Yes, but for him it doesn't matter, you see.

—

His girl is going to marry him anyhow.

Princess : (wide eyed) His *girl*. Socrates has a girl?!

Chanakaya : Why should you doubt that? He's a good-looking feller.

Princess : No, I meant if he had one and they were going steady we would have seen her with him sometime. She would have come to watch the rehearsals too.

Chanakaya : That's because his girl's not here. She's in Tundun.

Princess : Oh, he's marrying a Blitz, is he?

Chanakaya : Yeah. I guess it makes sense. He's Blitz himself, and wants to get a girl from back home.

Princess : (impatiently) Oh, what does it matter if he's Blitz or Bharatian. I MUST ask him about this girl of his.

Chanakaya : (sharply) No, don't!

Princess : Why?

Chanakaya : Why? Oh, because he *asked* me not to tell anyone.

Princess : But he told *you*.

Chanakaya : Yes, but that's because I'm his buddy. (sounds serious suddenly) Listen, you must not tell him I told you about this girl. He took a solemn promise from me not to tell anyone. It would break the poor guy's heart if he came to learn I was breaching confidences. It just somehow slipped out while talking to you just now.

Princess : (in a quiet tone) All right, all right, don't worry. I won't ask him anything.

Chanakaya : (looks at his watch) Oh, that reminds me. I'd better go and see what he's up to. He's supposed to go to collect the remaining furniture from the studio equipment people.

Princess : Furniture?

Chanakaya : (makes a gesture to indicate a space) We need another big table and some chairs. The General's asked both of us to set up the stage you know. Oh, here's the big man himself.

Enter General, who is dressed in a loose fitting *pathani* suit.

General : Hi, Princess. Hi, Channi. What's cooking?

Chanakaya : Nothing, boss. The Princess and I were just gassing. I was just leaving to go check about the stage furniture.

General : (looks around) Yeah, one more big table is needed there (points at a space). See if it's arrived. The responsibility is yours and Socrates. Where's our wise man, by the way?

Chanakaya : I saw him playing cards with Sutradhaar in the changing room a while ago. I'll go and check him out.

Exit Chanakaya

General : What's up, Princess? You're looking stressed out. Someone broke your heart.

Princess : (composing herself) No, general. It's a different problem.

General : Too many suitors then. That's in the play. (laughs)... and maybe real life as well, huh?

Princess : You're too smart, General. Got eyes at the back of your head, have you?

General : . . . and ears all over. Tell you what, Princess, why don't you reject the suitors, and take me overboard instead.

Princess : General, if you were only twenty years younger, I'd have jumped at the suggestion.

General : Not any more, huh? You're obviously someone who doesn't realize the value of experience. (shrugs) Well, your loss, my dear? So, who is it going to be?

Princess : I can't decide.

General : Just like in the play, the Princess could not decide

Princess : Yes, that's an amazing irony, isn't it? I think I must have taken my role too much to heart.

General : Listen, Princess, don't mess up this production. This is the big time play for all of us.

Princess : (seriously) I know that, General.

General : (looks at his watch) Hey, let's get dressed. There isn't much time.

Princess : Right, boss.

Exeunt The General And The Princess

A while later

Enter Socrates And Chanakaya

(Proceeding from the wing, they carry a wooden dining table on to the stage. After having placed the table at the appropriate place, they go back into the wings to fetch a few chairs, which they arrange around the table.)

Chanakaya : (breathing hard with the exertion) So how does it go, gow?

Socrates : Don't call me that!

Chanakaya : (repeats) *Gow*! (provocatively) Gow!!

Socrates : (aggressively) Don't call me gow! *Understand?!*

Chanakaya : What shall I call you then?

Socrates : Call me by my name. Socrates.

Chanakaya : That's only your stage name. What I can't understand is how the General chose you to play the part of Socrates.

Socrates : Well, you *can* believe that nobody could have forced him into the choice, can't you? ... and I could have refused the part too. It's a free world, isn't it?

Chanakaya : Humff. Refused?! Fat chance of that happening. And when you say free world, don't forget it was only fifty years ago you people were practically our slaves. If it hadn't been for Princess Ujala, you'd still be rotting.

Socrates : I don't deny her contribution, but you don't forget how so many people gave their lives for the cause. The truth is also that you couldn't bleed us anymore. We were completely impoverished as a nation at the time we got our freedom.

Chanakaya : So how do you explain that now its fifty years later and you're still the beggars you were. And now there are a whole lot of you trying to illegally migrate here so you can eat off the welfare system.

Socrates : (protests) I'm not an illegal immigrant!

Chanakaya : You got a scholarship from our Government to study theatre here, didn't you? You studied free, while I had to pay, and now you've landed this plum role while other better Bharatian actors are still struggling to pay off their study loans. Aren't you at least grateful?

Socrates : Not in the least.

Chanakaya : That's real shameless, I call it.

Socrates : You can take back your scholarship money if you like. I don't need it. Just give us back the riches you've been plundering from our land for two and a half centuries.

Chanakaya : You know the real reason why you people are poor. It's a basic flaw in your characters!

Socrates : Yeah, is that so?

Chanakaya : Plus some deep rooted cultural attitudes you need to change.

Socrates : I see only one thing Channi. The independence of Blighty has not in any way changed the attitude of some of the Bharatian people towards them. People like you, for instance, who continue to be as racist as before. And ignorant.

Chanakaya : That's one more trick you people have up your sleeve. Accuse us of racism at the drop of a hat

Socrates : Prejudice is what the ignorant use instead of reason. Let me test your ignorance, Channi. Can you tell me why our play's called Conquest At Noon?

Chanakaya : (smiling) You got me there! I haven't actually figured it out. It's not explained anywhere in the script ... and I guess I should know just in case any of the journalists quiz me about it after the show.

Socrates : That's the trouble with you people. We have to remember these things because we were a conquered people. You don't need to bother with such minor details. You were the victors.

Chanakaya : That's not the only reason you know. I mean to say we of the Bharatian empire conquered Blighty and so many other territories that you can't possibly expect us to remember all the small small details pertaining to each and every conquest we made. I bet if I asked you some detail pertaining to one of those other conquests you wouldn't know as well.

Socrates : Try me.

Chanakaya : (ignoring his reply) It's like if you were screwing only one woman regularly, you'd remember everything about her. The breast size, the mole on her right bum, but if you've got a bevy of chicks laying it out for you, you'd find it difficult to remember minor things about each one.

Socrates : (sarcastically) I have to hand it to you, Channi. Your analogies are always so fitting. You should have been a scriptwriter, do you realize? Acting is not really your forte.

Chanakaya : Trying to psyche me up, are you? I know all these slimy ways of you gows.

Socrates : Coming to your question about the title you obviously haven't read much history. The thing is that when the army of you brown people attacked us during the famous battle of Lassi, it was at the noon hour that your victory was accomplished. It was also at the noon hour that the attack was launched a week earlier. So the title is true in both senses. It was a conquest attempted at noon, which succeeded at noon.

Chanakaya : Oh, I see, but why did we choose to attack you at that particular time of day. Just a coincidence, I suppose.

Socrates : By no means. You see Blighty is an extremely cold country, as everyone knows. (goes to the world map and points it out) The Blitz people long for sunshine, which you have so much of in your country. When your people came in your ships from Bharat (draws an imaginary arc with his hand across the map to indicate the journey) you knew very well having studied the conditions thoroughly that noon was the time the sun was at its peak in Blighty and most of the Blitz soldiers threw off their armor and sunbathed. Just relaxed and tried to have the sun warm their bodies.

Chanakaya : Lazy bums. The lot of you. A battle for the country . . . and you want to warm your arses.

Socrates : (ignoring the comment) It wouldn't surprise me at all if the General wins the Fony award for best script and best direction as well.

Chanakaya : Yeah, the guy's a genius, but, well, he won't be in the running for the Fony award for best actor at any rate. That'll be only you and me as far as this play is concerned.

Socrate : (correcting him) You mean you *or* me.

Chanakaya : (snarling) Well, they'll break more than one record if they give it to you. The first gow to ever win a Fony award. That'll be the day. And I'll break something too that day. I'll break your fucking 'ead.

Socrates : Chanakaya, you jealous swine. I've read your history and I recall that there was a famous Chanakaya in the history of Maha Bharat even before the one who took part in Princess Ujala's *swayamvara.* A scheming, greedy fellow, if I remember correctly.

Chanakaya : Nonsense! He was a great diplomat. Speak for yourself. Socrates?! The prince of an island half the size of one of the smaller regions of Maha Bharat. And before him I too recall that imposter from one of our territories . . . who pretended to be wise.

Socrates : He didn't pretend. He *was* wise.

Chanakaya : (sarcastically) Just like you, I suppose. Fucking gow.

Socrates : Listen, if you call me gow, I'll call you (sputters with rage) . . . I'll call you . . . (suddenly excited) I *know* what I'll call you . . . a bloody *wog.* (laughs) *Wog.* That's right.

Chanakaya : (laughs) There's no such word.

Socrates : There **is** such a word. I just invented it. (repeats) Wog, wog.

Chanakaya : (smiles contemptuously) Amuse yourself. Listen, why don't you go back to your own country and act in plays in Tundun?

Socrates : Why don't *you*?

Chanakaya : Because I'm *brown,* understand. I'm in my own country. You're the refugee.

Socrates : Why did your people come to our peaceful island and subjugate us?

Chanakaya : You weren't peaceful! A savage people fighting with each other like cats and dogs. And even if we did some wrong things, now you have your own country, don't you? You should stick there.

Socrates : I would if you had.

Chanakaya : So you insist on milking us for what you can get, gow. Is that it?

Socrates : I'm only milking your conscience - which you for one don't possess - in any case.

Chanakaya : Right. So why don't you stop milking our consciences, and (folds his hands) *please* go back to your backwaters in Tundun.

Socrates : Why should I?

Chanakaya : Because you people are taking away the jobs from us brown people, can't you see? That's why! I'm not even sure if you're grateful to the General for having given you this important part to play.

Socrates : You're right. I'm not in the least grateful.

Chanakaya : Bastard! I knew it. I wish the General could hear you say this.

Socrates : I don't think it would affect him at all. You know Chanakaya, everyone is not like you. The General doesn't care for supplicants. He feels talent deserves a reward.

Chanakaya : Bullshit! The only reason you've got this part to play is because the General has this realism thing going and he wants an actual white man to play the part of Socrates. It goes down well with the critics.

Socrates : That's nonsense and you know it. I've had to work twice as hard as any brown actor to get this role. The General knows it . . . and so does the Princess. Where's the general, by the way?

Chanakaya : I dunno.

Socrates : He should be coming in any time for a last minute *dekho*, before the show begins.

Chanakaya : (pauses) He's probably busy screwing Milady.

Socrates : You mean Mohabattein.

Chanakaya : Yeah, she needs a new man every morning for breakfast. Why don't you take her yourself one of these days? I'm certain she'd be game.

Socrates : You know in this respect I rather like the attitude of earlier Bharatians. I'm not very much in favor of these . . .

Chanakaya : Jest for one fucking night, you mean. Yeah, I know what you mean. (guffaws) Should be for at least a week.

Socrates : One night stands, I think you call them.

Chanakaya : (musing) One night *stands*. Well, that's what gows are famous for, aren't they? Promiscuity. Fucking around. Except that we Bharatians have also been affected by your stupid gow culture.

Socrates : (bitterly) It has been one of the causes for our defeat.

Chanakaya : That's bloody right. This reminds me, why don't you whites stick to your own women, damn it.

Socrates : Why didn't you browns stick to yours? You used our women and us for three centuries, didn't you?

Chanakaya : We gave them more respect than you did.

Socrates : More respect! You just used them when you could.

Chanakaya : Haven't you heard Ruddy Baba's poem 'Cardiff Bay'?

(starts singing)

By the old Welshy Cathedral, lookin' lazy at the sea, There's a Blighted girl a-setting, and I know she thinks of me; For the wind is in the Willows, and the church bells they say; 'Come you back, you Prustian soldier, come you back to Cardiff Bay!'

Come you back to Cardiff Bay,
Where the old Flotilla lay;
Can't you 'ear their paddles clunkin' from Bridgewater to Cardiff Bay
On the road to Cardiff Bay
Where the flyin' seagulls play
An' the rain pours down and there's thunder when rough weather 'crost the Bay!
'Er winter coat was yaller, and 'er little skirt was green,
An' her name was Ang-Her-Rad, jes' the same as the Welshy Queen[5]
An' I seed her first a-smokin' of a whacking white cheroot,
An' wasting soulful kisses on a wooden painted crucifix;
Bloomin' 'fix with a trapeze artist,
Wot they called the Great Lord Christ
Plucky lot she cared for such 'fixes when I kissed 'er where she stud!

On the road to Cardiff Bay…[6]

Socrates : You don't even realize how offensive that last stanza can be to a religious person.

Chanakaya : Come now, don't be so uptight. Listen, I believe you've been propositioning the princess.

Socrates : (equably) Well, so have you.

Chanakaya : I'm serious about her.

Socrates : So am I.

---

5. There was indeed a Welsh Queen by this name.

6. This is an adaptation of Rudyard Kipling's famous poem on Burma, titled 'Mandalay' Last part of the second stanza in that poem reads:
An' wasting Christian kisses on an 'eathen idol's foot;
Bloomin' idol made o' mud—
Wot they called the Great God Budd—
Plucky lot she cared for idols when I kisser 'er where she stud!
On the road to Mandalay…

Chanakaya : (furious) Listen, just don't try messing around . . . .

Enter General, now attired in military uniform, a pencil thin Hitler like moustache painted over his lips. He is smoking a cigarette through an ivory holder.

General : Cut it out, you guys. What the devil are you quarreling about? Show's going to begin in fifteen minutes, and you haven't even put on your dresses. Don't you idiots realize that this is the biggest chance you have in your life to become superstars? (peremptorily) Where's the Princess?

Socrates : She's in the dressing room, getting made up.

General : Women! They take such a long time, don't they? (sees that the throne is unstable) Hey, just let's move this throne a bit to the right. It might just fall off from here. We don't want the Princess to look like a fool.

(They all push it a bit to the right.)

Chanakaya : (looking at the throne) It looks quite impressive, doesn't it?

General : It had better. We've had to pay a fortune for it. It's an exact replica of the famous Peacock Throne, which has come down to succeeding kings since the time of Emperor Karan Karim. (notices that the curtains are not drawn) Bloody phools!! Do either of you realize that you haven't even bothered to pull the stage curtains. The audience has already come into the auditorium, and settled into their seats. You jokers haven't even pulled the curtains.

Chanakaya : It's all because of this gow.

Socrates : No, it's because of you, you wog.

(They start to scuffle)

General : (shouts) Break it up, I said! And pull the curtains now at least, for Sant Kabir's sake!

Do you want the audience to start throwing rotten apples at us?

(As if on cue, a couple of rotten apples land on to the stage)

Socrates : I know what we can do! We can pretend that it's not that we forgot to pull the curtain, but, as a matter of fact, all this conversation going on is part of the play.

Chanakaya : (addresses the audience) He's really a wise guy, isn't he?

General : (peremptorily) No, there is something in what he says.

Chanakaya : Come on director *sahib*. Audiences are very intelligent these days. You can't fool them so easily. You try and cheat them; they'll throw rotten *tomatoes* at you.

As if on cue, a dozen rotten tomatoes land on to the stage

Chanakaya : See! I told you!!

General : (screams) *Do* something, someone!

Socrates : Look, as I was explaining to this oaf Channi he should explain to the audience . . . here let me do it . . . (loudly) Ladies and Gentlemen! Welcome to the first day and the first show of CONQUEST AT NOON. This scene here is part of the play. It's *not* as if we forgot to draw the curtain . . . Now a selection of more rotten fruit lands on to the stage.

Socrates : (shouts to someone in the wings) Pull the bloody curtain, will you?!

Curtain Falls

Scene 3

An elderly man dressed simply in *bundi*[7] and *dhoti*[8] comes on stage, in front of the curtain, which has yet to lift, carrying three boards mounted on folding stands and sets them up next to himself. On the first one is depicted a large map of the world, the second board shows up a map of the United Kingdom and the third one is an ordinary blackboard.

Sutradhaar: Dear friends, all of you who are gathered here today. I am a sutradhaar. What, you may well ask, or rather who, is a *sutradhaar*. Very simple. A *sutradhaar* is quite literally a literary device used by playwrights to introduce certain other characters as well as situations in a play. But mine today is a double role. I am no ordinary *sutradhaar*, you see.

In my other incarnation, I am Sanjay, younger brother to a king – and no ordinary king at that. It was the Jahanpanah himself, direct descendant of the Emperor Karan Karim and the inheritor of one of the most powerful and long lasting dynasties of the world, the Limshumdin dynasty. And indeed shortly in the very next scene that follows you shall see me in that role of Sanjay, brother of Jahanpanah, and even more importantly great uncle, advisor and confidante to Princess Ujala. But for now, I am in my lesser role of a humble *sutradhaar*.

Do you know what is special about the humble *sutradhaar*? He is someone who has *eyes*, but each one of you too has eyes, you will no doubt say, so what's the difference? The difference, dear friends, is that I have *big* eyes, (blinks rapidly twice). They don't look so big to you? I was only speaking metaphorically, or is it metaphysically?

---

7. A half vest, commonly worn by peasants in India.

8. A cloth draped around the waist, commonly worn by peasants in India.

What I mean to say is that I can see *everything* that is going on. I can see for instance that that little boy sitting in the last row of the auditorium is troubling his mother very much. (expectedly the audience will turn back to see who it is) So can you? But I can also see that this gentleman sitting in the front row, yes this gentleman in the blue[9] shirt, has left his wife at home, has lied to her that he is working late in office, and has come to see this show with his secretary. Can you see that?

I can see all of you as you were an hour ago, sitting in your homes. The gentlemen coming home from office, having that much deserved cup of tea, then going for a shower, yes I can see the ladies too having their bath. I can see you taking off your work-clothes and changing into evening dress, into those lovely silk *sarees* and skirts, I can see under those skirts . . .

I can hear some of you muttering, "Lucky swine!" (turns serious) No, my friends, I am not that lucky. I have seen such terrible things happening, such violence, such murders, such rapes, such pillage and looting that I would much prefer it if I was like one of you sitting out there, unable to see anything – anything at all.

Let me get to my appointed task. I am right now before you only as a *sutradhaar,* but I may sound like a professor of history – *sutradhaars* often do - who will tell you a little bit more than you already know about the Maha Bharat Empire. History lessons are terribly boring, aren't they? So I promise to be as brief as I can.

(assumes a professorial tone) The first important period from our point of view are the years 1556 up till 1605. (he writes down these dates with a piece of chalk on the blackboard).

In 1556 there took place the historic matrimonial union between the Princess Sultana of the M dynasty with Prince Ramish Ramzan of the P dynasty. Consequent upon this marriage there took place a merger of the two major dynasties in Maha Bharat, for the M dynasty controlled the North and the P controlled the South. Shortly thereafter, due to certain

9. Or whatever color it really is. The actor will improvise.

uneventful deaths in the two families, this royal couple assumed the duties of King and Queen. King Ramish Ramzan did not however reign for long, and suffered from a fatal illness in the third year of his reign.

While the King was still alive Queen Sultana gave birth to two sons, Prince Kabir, the elder one and Prince Karan Karim. An astrologer prophesized that one son would become a great mystic and the other a great warrior. The prophesy came true, but not in the way people expected.

Prince Kabir who otherworldly from his earliest years, chose not to marry and was profoundly interested in the deeper issues, of finding out the meaning of life, the nature of our existence. In the short thirty-five years that were accorded to him, he consolidated the two great world religions of that time and created the powerful Shakti movement.

Two years after his death, the aging and widowed Queen Sultana suffered a massive heart attack and the young Prince Karan Karim ascended to the throne.

This period 1586 up till 1605 coincides with the period of the reign of the Great Limshumdin, Karan Karim who was the Emperor of Maha Bharat, but you know that already? It was an exciting epoch, for with the coming of the great mystic Sant Kabir and the birth of the great Shakti movement, the two great world religions of the time were unified. The political consequences of this religious union were tremendous, for it made it possible for the Emperor to bring together the North and the South of the continent for the first time, and establish a single, united Maha Bharat (points to India on the world map).

For the next two hundred and fifty years, that is to say from the year 1605 up till 1856 (writes this period out in chalk on the blackboard), it was a period of tremendous scientific and industrial progress in Maha Bharat which was contemporaneous – that is the right expression, I believe - with the conquest of a great deal of overseas territory. The subjugation of the island of Blighty in 1757 during the famous Battle of Lassi was a major landmark of these developments (points to England on the map of the UK). Later historians described Blighty as 'the jewel in the crown' of the Maha

Bharatian Empire, and it's subjugation set the seal on further conquests by later Bharatian monarchs across the sub-continental region (makes a circular movement on the map to indicate Europe on the world map). Now, these other territories – Sufrika [10], Farrakas,[11] Myna,[12] and other such areas do not really concern us. They were developed civilizations in their own right, had their own kings and queens, and we did not bother much about them, except to send the occasional ambassador, and to receive theirs.

Next. (a dramatic pause here) 1857. (writes down the date on the blackboard) A **very** important date. There is mutiny in Blighty. The Blitz (points on the map[13]), the Bots (points on the map[14]) and the Welshy (points on the map[15]) came together in an attempt to throw out the foreign power, that's us. The Virish people on a neighbouring island (points on the map[16]) however come to the rescue of the Bharatian army – for they had ancient enmities with the Blitz – and with their support, which was indeed crucial, we managed to crush the rebellion. The quelling of this rebellion was accompanied by the siege and destruction of the city of Tundun. There was tremendous slaughter, arson and looting of the treasures of that ancient city. Before the mutiny was crushed some of our Bharatian ladies were raped by the natives (pauses here, looking sorrowful).

We now come to relatively recent times. 1930 up till 1935. (writes it down on the blackboard) Five important years. Pay close attention now. I can see some of you nodding off.

The emperor of Maha Bharat during this period was Jahanpanah, direct descendant of Emperor Akbar, in short form sometimes simply called JP. Who were the other important historical figures of this time? Apart from JP himself, (and yours truly) there was his prime minister, Behru, the Army Commander General Brandy, and his lieutenant Col Mossambi. Mainly moderate leaders such as Birchbill and Sunpearl Lion led the Blitz independence movement at that time.

10. Points to Africa
11. Points to the Americas
12. Points to China
13. To England
14. To Scotland
15. To Wales
16. To Ireland

There also existed some militant factions, who also participated and lent energy to the movement. The killing of militant leader Devtee Lion, founder of the Blitz Krieg during the forcible sterilization campaign of 1935 sparked off nation wide protests. The Jahanpanah's only son, JP Junior and his wife Nityamma are killed when some militants plant a bomb in their carriage. The only possible successor to the throne can now be Princess Ujala, granddaughter of the emperor. (pauses)

The independence struggle of the Blitz people had been cruelly crushed by repressive techniques employed by JP, but within a quarter century JP, Birchbill and Behru all pass away. JP himself survived both Birchbill and Behru but ultimately passed away in 1942. After his death, his granddaughter Princess Ujala is crowned as the new Empress of Maha Bharat. And then barely five years later on the 15th of August 1947, in the week before the princess turns twenty six, following a two thousand year old tradition, a *swayamvara* is held in which the princess will choose her future life partner. For the first time in recorded history, a *white* prince, Prince Socrates is permitted to participate as a suitor-candidate in the royal *swayamvara.*

But why am I telling you all this? Don't you know it yourselves? Didn't you read all about it in the history books at school? Well . . . No harm done if I just refreshed your memory a bit, is there? (pauses)

I'll leave you now, my friends to witness this grand ceremony and also to see me in my other incarnation . . .

Exit Sutradhaar

Scene 4

(The same set as the final arranged set in the previous scene. The set is empty except for an attendant, seated at a distance from the door. An elderly man with a long white beard, dressed in regal robes is seated in an elaborately designed chair just next to the Peacock throne.)

There is a knock on the door. The attendant hops towards the door.

Sanjay : No, wait, I'll open the door. It's an important day and it could be an important message from one of the princes. He goes to the door, and opens it.

Outside, there is standing a fierce looking man with a long white beard, a red *tikka* adorning his forehead, dressed in flowing white robes, and next to him are two young similarly attired disciples.

Sanjay : Welcome Guruji, welcome! What a wonderful surprise! I suppose you have come to attend the *swayamvara*.

Guruji : Listen to me my son. I have not attended any celebratory activities for the last thirty years, and I am too old to change now.

Sanjay : Oh, but Guruji please be seated at least.

Guruji : No, Sanjay, I have not come here to sit. There is something very important I need to discuss with you.

Sanjay : Oh, but Guruji, you should not have bothered. I am your humble servant. You should have simply sent for me.

Guruji : Under normal circumstances I would not have made this journey from the forest to the capital. I am ninety years old and my legs are not very strong anymore. I was compelled to come because one of my disciples gave me some very disturbing news yesterday.

Sanjay : (mystified) Disturbing news?! I cannot imagine what that could be. Our people are happier with the Princess than they were with the last three monarchs, and in our overseas dominions in Blighty and neighboring territories too there has been peace and quiet the last two weeks.

Guruji : What I have heard is even more disturbing than any possible disturbances you have just alluded to. It concerns certain goings on in the royal palace.

Sanjay : In the palace? Whatever could that be . . .

Guruji : Is it not true that the Princess's *swayamvara* will take place an hour from now?

Sanjay : Yes, yes, Guruji. The announcement of this was made in the Royal Gazette two weeks ago. I personally ensured that a special intimation of this was dispatched to you.

Guruji : I am not complaining that I was not informed about the event, Sanjay – the whole country knows about the *swayamvara*. It is something far far more serious that was not communicated to me.

Sanjay : Yes, Guruji?

Guruji : Is it true that from a list of a hundred princes there are in all finally four royal suitors who have been invited from the various provinces of Maha Bharat.

Sanjay : Guruji, there are in all five princes who have been invited.

Guruji : (in a triumphant tone) So what I have heard

is correct. Who pray is this fifth man? (pauses significantly) Is he white?

Sanjay : (understanding now) Yes, Guruji, but he is a prince.

Guruji : White man a prince?! How can that be? All the whites have been subjugated long ago. From where will a white prince appear? From the sky?

Sanjay : Guruji, there is a small island near Blighty which our forces never captured. The last attempt was made seventy-five years ago, but failed. Thereafter we left the people from that island alone.

Guruji : Utter and complete nonsense!! That island was left alone because it was of no use to us. I remember the battle. It took place in my early youth. Our army was ordered to withdraw, because it was realized that the island was not in any case worth our while. There was something wrong with the soil. It was all rocky mountain, but no minerals. Plantations were inconceivable. So the attempt was abandoned.

Sanjay : (sounding humble) I bow to your superior knowledge, Guruji, but all the same this means that the island was sovereign and under the rules Royal Prince Socrates is eligible to apply for the hand of our Princess.

Guruji : By no means. We are the interpreters of the religious texts. Our advice should have been sought in this regard. This white man – is he not by race a Blitz, since the island is so close to Blighty?

Sanjay : He is, Guruji.

Guruji : Does he not speak the same language as them?

Sanjay : He does, but He also speaks prustian, the major bhartian language as well as I do, and

With A Perfect Accent.

Guruji : (raising his voice now) Silence! Is he not a believer in primitive religion?

Sanjay : (in a trembling tone) That may be so, Guruji, but he is well educated. In his application for being considered as a suitor, he has accepted the overladyship of our Empress, as it might otherwise appear unseemly for him to compete with the other princes from Maha Bharat. The prince does not practice his primitive religion, and has made it clear in his request for being considered a worthy suitor that he would be quite happy to get married according to traditional Bharatian rites and customs. I think – though I cannot say so with certainty - he could be persuaded to convert.

Guruji : (thunders) What did you say?! Conversion? This white man follow our customs! No, no, this is not permitted. The white man is like an animal. In five lifetimes they will not be able to comprehend the teachings of the great mystic Kabir.

Sanjay : With respect, Guruji, if you meet this Prince you would feel differently perhaps – not that there is any danger at all of the Princess accepting him as her life partner.

Guruji : Do you not realize Sanjay, that our religion itself will be endangered if the Princess was to accept this barbarian as her husband. Does she not realize her responsibilities? She is not only the Empress – we call her Princess only as an act of endearment on account of her youth and beauty – she is also the Head of our Great Temple.

Sanjay : (hastily) There is no danger of the Princess accepting the white prince, Guruji. It is my feeling that this may be a political move on the part of the Princess to quell rebellion in Blighty.

Guruji : (astonished) A political move?! Why, of course! This had not crossed my mind. Could this indeed be the reason for this strange decision?

Sanjay : I believe so, Guruji. Of late the Princess has been taking great interest in our political affairs, and her recent political decisions have displayed extraordinary maturity.

Guruji : I see that she devotes a fair amount of energy to charitable causes as well.

Sanjay : Yes. The Princess has two major interests, Guruji. Politics or affairs of the state should I say, and secondly or even more importantly helping the poor and needy.

Guruji : I see that she did not go to open the flower exhibition at the Shalimar Gardens last summer, but sent someone else instead.

Sanjay : Yes, she considers such events to be frivolous and meaningless – although she loves flowers.

Guruji : She is very practical and down to earth then?

Sanjay : There is a mystical and poetic side to her as well, Guruji. And I should have mentioned a third major interest. The princess loves philosophy and philosophical discourse.

Guruji : Indeed! She should come to see me more often then in that case. Anyhow, to move to the subject under discussion. I take it that there is no danger of our Princess actually marrying this white savage?

Sanjay : (in a reassuring tone) None whatsoever, Guruji. None whatsoever.

Guruji : (relaxes now) I am greatly relieved to hear that, my son. Well, in that case I had better be going now.

Sanjay : No, no, Guruji. Please be seated. The Princess will be coming down shortly. I will just send for some *sherbet*. (shouts) Khidmatgar!

Guruji : No, no, this is not necessary. If it was necessary I would have stayed to speak to the Princess, but with your explanation I am at ease. It is evident that he will not be chosen, and this is only a political stratagem to keep the savages peaceful and well behaved. I will take your leave now. You will be busy with the preparations. Do convey my blessings to her Royal Highness.

Sanjay bows down, and touches the Guru's feet.

Guruji : Listen my son, God forbid, should anything go wrong in today's contest, in that event . . . (whispers something in Sanjay's ear)

Sanjay : Yes, Guruji. I appreciate your faith in me.

Guruji : May God grant you a long and happy life, my son. Come, *chelas,* let us go.

Exit Guruji

Sanjay : (speaks to himself, while mopping his brow) I myself don't know quite what this girl is up to. Guruji is perfectly right. Why on earth did she have to include Prince Socrates name in the finalized list of suitors? I'm only hoping it was a political move on her part, for it is true that of late she has begun to take a great interest in matters of state.

Enter Princess (at the top of the staircase)

Princess : (coming down the staircase) Who was that *chachaji*? Weren't you talking to someone just now? I could hear voices.

Sanjay : It was the Head Priest, my dear.

Princess : Oh, why did he come?

Sanjay : He was upset on account your including the candidature of the White Prince amongst the final list of suitors. I had advised against his inclusion, if you remember.

Princess : Why, it's a girl's privilege to make her choice

in these matters. Are the two of you going to instruct me on whom to include and whom not to?

Sanjay : You don't understand, my dear. Guruji feels the Blitz are savage.

Princess : Did not the great Kabir say that all men were equal?

Sanjay : Of course he did, my dear, but . . .

Princess : Come, *chachaji*, what's done cannot be undone. And I as the Empress will not countenance the springing up of any rival centers of power. Such ambitions do not behove those who have taken on a religious mantle upon themselves, and must I feel be nipped in the bud.

Sanjay : You misjudge him, my dear. (changes the subject) You're looking wonderful, might I say.

Princess : Thank you, *chachu*. The hairdresser has done a good job, but I still need to change into my *swayamvara* dress and put on all that jewelry. (she descends the staircase by now and gives him a big hug) I wish my parents could have been here today. (wipes a tear) Well, at least you're there. Someone I can have complete trust in.

Enter Footman

Footman : Your Highness, the three chief cabinet ministers have come to see you together with Army Commander, General Chaudhury

Princess : At this time?! Oh yes, I'm forgetting. I had called them myself at this time only.

Sanjay : Why today my dear and at this time? You could have met them at the Secretariat.

Princess : Oh *chachaji*, the Defense Minister said he needed me to sign some Government Order urgently and that it would take only five minutes, so I said come along to the palace itself an hour before the ceremony and we'll get it done with, whatever it is. Oh yes, please footman, please show them in. Come, Uncle, let's be seated.

Sanjay : You deal with them, my dear. I'll just go and check that all the arrangements are in order

Exit Sanjay

The Princess Sits Down On The Peacock Throne.

Enter The Defense Minister, Mr Gundu, Mr Sobhraj, Mr Dang And General Chaudhury.

Defence Minister : Sorry to disturb you at such a time, Your Highness.

Princess : Not at all Minister. I recall that I myself had suggested the time when you said it was a two-minute job. Please come in gentleman, and be seated. I see the Army Commander is also here. It seems to be something more important than I had imagined. Some tea, perhaps? Khidmatgar!

Mr Dang : No, Your Highness, we will not take any refreshment. As a matter of fact we are sorry to have intruded upon your privacy at such a time.

Princess : Not at all, not at all. Come, tell me, what is the matter?

Mr Shobhraj : The thing is, Your Highness, that we urgently needed your signatures on some Government orders. (pushes some papers towards her, and indicates a cross mark) Here, Your Highness. At the place where the cross is marked.

Mr Dang : (whips out a pen) Here, Your Highness.

Princess : (takes the pen) Well, what is this document? It's very lengthy. It looks like some new complicated law. I was under the impression this was something very minor.

Defence
Minister : Your Highness, it is a very small matter.

Princess : Minister, you know perfectly well that I do not pass any law or ordinance unless I have read it carefully and understood all the implications. You should have sent me these papers a week ago.

Def. Min. : I'm sorry, Your Highness, it won't happen again. As a matter of fact the Legislative Department got it prepared only yesterday.

Princess : (wearily)Well, all right, there is no time for me to read it now, but tell me in a nutshell, what is this all about.

Defence
Minister : Nothing very major, Your Highness. Just some tax amendments, whereby a few new taxes are sought to be imposed.

Princess : What are these taxes being levied upon?

Mr Dang : On cloth, soap, electricity, water, and baby food, Your Highness.

Mr Shobhraj : We hope to be able to raise some three hundred million as a result of this.

Princess : Don't you know that taxes such as the one's you are proposing will affect the poor people the most.

Defence
Minister : Well, yes, Your Highness, but we need the money urgently.

Princess : Why, the Finance Minister told me only the other day that our coffers are full.

Defence
Minister : That's true, Your Highness, but as the Defense Minister of this nation, it is my considered view that we need to establish at least three more armament factories.

Princess : Armament factories?! We don't need any more

armament factories. We need to have more housing for the poor and the homeless, more hospital services, more financial assistance for the people living in wretched conditions in our overseas dominions.

Defence Minister : Your Highness, it is necessary for the nations security that we establish these factories.

Princess : Nonsense, Defense Minister. As it is, I believe that the defense budget needs to be cut back.

Mr Dang : We could be attacked by some other power, Your Highness. This expenditure is necessary.

Princess : Why do States act like . . . what's the word? . . . Gladiators... Yes. Gladiators eager to posture and get locked into mortal combat with other States? No one has defeated our army in five hundred years. It is not likely to take place in the near future. We need our armaments, like all nations do, but it is my clear impression that we already have many more arms and deadly weapons as compared with any other power on earth. What is the position, General?

General Chaudhury : Your Highness, at the present moment in terms of weaponry we possess five times what any other military power has.

Princess : There, Minister, what did I tell you?

Mr Dang : Your Highness, we need at least ten times.

Princess : Nonsense! Go away! I will not punish the poor people of this land any more. As a matter of fact, I'm beginning to think that we should stop the manufacture of some of our weapons. What is that weapon, General, which is frequently quite small in size, which is hidden in the fields of an enemy nation. When an unsuspecting villager walks past, the poor fellow just gets his legs blown off.

General Chaudhury : I believe Your Highness is alluding to land mines.

Princess : Yes, that's the word for it! My view, Defense Minister is that rather than establish new factories, we should instead be thinking of closing down such factories completely which manufacture weapons such as these.

Defense Minister : Your Highness is joking!

Princess : (raises her eyebrows) Joking?! Certainly not! I do not trifle on such issues.

General Chaudhury : I suggest we take leave of Her Highness now. She has made plain her view on the proposed bill.

Princess : Yes, General, thank you. We will continue this discussion sometime next week perhaps. For the moment, you will have to excuse me. The ceremony will start soon.

Mr Dang : Please Your Highness.

Mr Shobhraj : Beg your leave, highness.

Defense Minister : Sorry to have troubled you, Your Highness. Of course your decision is final.

Exeunt Defense Minister, Mr Shobhraj, Mr Dang And General Chaudhury

Sanjay : Thank God they've gone. Time is getting ahead of us. (shouts) Khidmadgar!

Khidmatgar : Yes, Sir.

Sanjay : Are the tables fully laid out for the guests?

Khidmatgar : Oh Yes, Sir.

Sanjay : And the sherbets are ready and sufficiently chilled?

Khidmatgar : Yes, Hazoor.

Princess : And The Kebabs?

Khidmatgar : They are being grilled, Your Royal Highness, and will be ready in five minutes so they could be served piping hot. I believe Great Uncle is double checking everything.

Enter Sanjay

Sanjay : Everything is in order. (looks at his watch) Are you ready, Princess? It is time now. The princes will be here anytime.

Princess : Let me go and change into my dress then. I'll be done in half an hour. If I'm late, will you show the princes in, Uncle?

Sanjay : Of course my dear.

Scene 5

The same setting as in the very first scene, with minor modifications. A placard has been placed which proudly announces 'THE *SWAYAMVARA* OF PRINCESS UJALA'. Five princes are seated around the tables, drinking goblets of red wine served by liveried bearers (waiters). The seat at the head of the table is vacant. These princes include Prince Socrates wearing a blue *achkan* and Prince Chanakaya in a black *bandgala*. The princes all seem to be listening keenly to Prince Veerappa, whose royal attire is somewhat military, and who from his gestures appears to be speaking of his physical prowess in the battlefield.

Princess Ujala dressed gorgeously in a chiffon *saree*, a jeweled tiara gleaming on her forehead, is seated on the Peacock Throne at a slight elevation from the floor, and seated next to her is her great-uncle SANJAY with whom she is talking. This arrangement is towards the audience so that their conversation can be heard (the princess and her uncle's). From time to time the Head Waiter approaches the Princess and she is seen to be giving directions. She seems to enjoy supervising the affair, taking care that no one's glass is empty, etc. After a while she goes back to sit with her Uncle.

Sanjay : Everything seems to have gone smoothly so far. The newspapers were trying very hard to have a representative allowed in, but I flatly refused. A *swayamvara* is essentially a very private ceremony.

Princess : I wonder who is the interviewer and who is the interviewee.

Sanjay : Certainly, it is entirely your choice, Princess. You may reject any suitor (indeed you will accept any one) but as regards the Princes, their very presence here today signifies their assent.

Princess : Isn't it unfair? Why don't we hold *swayamvaras* for men?

Sanjay : Men and women are not equal, which is not to say that either one of the sexes is any less. They are different however. It does not behove our tradition to have a ceremony where the women feel disappointed at having been rejected. The men can feel rejected, though they must be valiant enough to overcome their feelings.

Princess : Yet not every woman has a *swayamvara*

Sanjay : Men and women were not created equal, and neither were all women, or indeed men. Amongst women it is only the most beautiful, the most intelligent, the most accomplished who can have the possibility of holding a *swayamvara*. But enough discussion, my child. I believe it is time to begin the ceremony.

(Sanjay stands up and claps his hands twice. The murmur at the dining tables dies down)

Sanjay : (loudly announces) Welcome to you, my Princes!! I hope you are all well settled and refreshed. I will name all the suitors gathered today, although I believe you would know each other in any case and those who did not would have introduced themselves. Gathered today for on the auspicious occasion of the *swayamvara* of our beloved Princess are the following suitors: Prince Chanakaya from Patliputra, Prince Veerappa from Southern Bharat, Prince Soumitra from Bongland, , Prince Suleiman from Peshawarbad, and Prince Socrates from Blighty!!

You are all well aware that according to procedures laid down in our ancient texts, in the *swayamvara* each suitor is to have the opportunity to speak briefly with the lady for whose benefit the *swayamvara* is being held. However in a slight variation of this procedure, the Princess shall ask a single question and each one of you shall be given an opportunity to answer it best as you can.

Now, Princess...

(At this juncture, the Princess rises and goes to the tables where she does a dignified *namaste* to those seated there – which gesture is politely returned by the guests- and then goes and stands next to her uncle)

Princess : Thank you for coming. I have a simple question to ask you. Do you believe in an afterlife? If so, why so? If not, why not?

Sanjay : Will each of the Princes respond in turn? If the Princess has any further question that arises from your answer, you will of course be expected to respond. Who would like to go first?

(There is a moment of silence. The Princes look at each other, as if to ask who should begin. Prince Veerappa raises his hand.)

Princess : I have heard much about your amazing military exploits, Prince Veerappa. I somehow guessed that you would be the first to speak.

P. Veerappa : (bows his head graciously) Thank you. (pauses) Princess, I *do* believe in an afterlife. After all, it is mentioned in our most ancient scriptures, is it not?

Princess : Yes, but did the Great Kabir have something to say on it?

P. Veerappa : I don't think so.

Princess : Then why do you believe?

P. Veerappa : I base my belief on the ancient scriptures, which Sant Kabir did not contradict in this respect.

Princess : Any other reason?

P.Veerappa : No, Your Highness.

Princess : Thank you, Prince Veerappa.

(There is a moment of silence, then the next prince, Prince Soumitra speaks up)

P. Soumitra : As my friend Prince Veerappa just remarked, the Great Kabir was himself silent on the subject. I believe he was silent because while he actually did not believe there was any afterlife, he did not want to say so.

Princess : (in an amused tone) And why pray, according to you, did he keep quiet, when he did otherwise speak so extensively on so many subjects?

P. Soumitra : Your Highness must not forget that this was a time of consolidation of two different – though not always conflicting – spiritual worldviews. Politics is the art of the possible, Your Highness knows this very well, and the Great Kabir did not wish to stir up a controversy. It is for this reason, that while he did not actually believe in an afterlife at all, he did not want to contract the two prevalent spiritual worldviews on this point, who were both agreed that there was indeed an afterlife.

Princess : And you, Prince, what do you believe?

P. Soumitra : I believe that the Great Kabir believed that there was no afterlife, and I too like him do so believe. It is only this life we have, and we should make the most of it.

(There is a moment of silence)

Princess : Thank you, Prince Soumitra.

P. Suleiman : *(begins speaking)* I do not agree with my friend, Prince Soumitra, that the great Himu did not actually believe in an afterlife, or with Prince Veerappa that he did believe in one.

He was silent, we know this.

My friend says that politics is the art of the possible, but Sant Kabir was no politician.

He was a Master, and what he taught and practiced was the art of the impossible. I do not believe that the great fusion he created was the result of a cold calculation of what would be acceptable to the masses, and what would not. He was silent. The meaning is clear. He did not believe, he did not disbelieve, and I too am like him.

Princess : In other words, you do not believe in an afterlife?

P. Suleiman : And I do not also disbelieve in one.

Princess : So it could exist then according to you?

P. Suleiman : Yes.

Princess : You grant the possibility?

P. Suleiman : I do. I also grant the possibility that it does not.

Princess : In other words, you do not know.

P. Suleiman : And therefore I do not believe.

Princess : Well, that's very honest and straightforward, I must say. Thank you, Prince Suleiman. (glances around)

P. Socrates : I would like to speak now

Princess : Please go ahead, Prince.

P. Socrates : I believe in rebirth and I have a very strong argument for it.

Princess : Yes?

P. Socrates : In physics, we are told that one of the basic

principles is that matter cannot be created or destroyed.

Princess : Yes, that is true.

P. Socrates : Well, if matter cannot be created or destroyed according to the laws of physics, I propose that according to the laws of metaphysics life also cannot be created or destroyed.

Princess : Interesting. Very interesting. You say life cannot be created also? What about the babies who keep getting born?

P. Socrates : From the outside this appears like the creation of life, but in reality it is just that the life force has at that very instant left another body. It is not creation, but merely the migration of the life force from one body to another.

Princess : Then how do you explain the phenomenal growth in population these last two centuries, when advances in medicine have raised life expectancy?

P. Socrates : It is the human ego, which grades the life force in human beings as something special, Princess. In reality it is not so. Along side the growth in human population there has been a proportionate reduction in the number of animal species, of plant varieties and so on and forth.

Princess : Oh, I see. Your point is that the sum total of *all* life, animal, human or vegetable remains the same.

P. Socrate : Exactly!

Princess : Well, do you have any proof of this proposal of yours that life cannot be created or destroyed? Or is it just a proposal?

P. Socrates : I do have proof your Highness. Of a kind.

Princess : And what do you mean by the latter

statement?

P. Socrates : I mean of course that all proofs, whether in geometry or in metaphysics are based on some things we like to call assumptions. And my proof needs only one assumption, which no one will seek to challenge here.

Princess : And what is that assumption?

P. Socrates : My assumption is that matter exists and so does life. And matter is dead.

Princess : Why, no one would challenge such an assumption?!

P. Socrates : That is what I meant Your Highness. When I say matter is dead and completely separate from life, I would also like this to mean that matter can never ever become life, because the two are entirely separate.

Princess : All right, we accept this assumption, and its implication. And so, what do you deduce from these two assumptions?

P. Socrates : There is a method of proof used in mathematics, whereby you make an assumption, and then show how that assumption will result in consequences, which are simply fantastic. By this method of reasoning you succeed in proving that your assumption is false.

Princess : I don't quite follow, but do go on.

P. Socrates : Now I will make a third assumption and show how it is quite false.

Princess : And that assumption is...?

P. Socrates : I assume that life can be destroyed, that is to say, reduced to matter.

Princess : Fair enough. And how is this impossible? It keeps getting destroyed everyday, as far as we observe and understand it.

P. Socrates : If a single life could be destroyed, then

theoretically all life could also be destroyed.

Princess : Of course that is true.

P. Socrates : Well, then *if* all life *did* get destroyed...

Princess : Yes?

P. Socrates : It could never be created again.

Princess : Why not?

P. Socrates : Because what would remain would be matter, and we just now agreed that matter shall be defined as being so completely separate from the life force, that it itself could never create life. For if matter was potential life, then where and how would we distinguish between the two?

Princess : All right. Accepted. And therefore you say this means that all life was never destroyed?

P. Socrates : If life could be destroyed, then one must realistically suppose that it would at one point of time have been completely destroyed.

Princess : Why must one realistically suppose this?

P. Socrates : Because, Your Highness, we live in eternity, and in the eternity of time that lies behind us, it would have sometime happened, if it could happen.

Princess : (is thoughtful) Very interesting. Your proof, I mean. (looks around) Well... this has been quite a brainstorming session, hasn't it gentlemen? Who's left?

P. Chanakaya : Your Highness, if I may be permitted to speak.

Princess : Of course, Prince! We are most anxious to hear your opinion.

P. Chanakaya : I do not believe in an after life and I have my own reasons for it.

Princess : So you rely on your own mind, and do not

accept necessarily what our forbears might have had to say on the subject.

P. Chanakaya : That is right, Your Highness.

Princess : And what are the reasons, Prince?

P. Chanakaya : What is a man? Or for that matter, what is a woman? (pauses significantly) We are, dear Princess, a bundle of memories, impressions, and relationships. I am myself, like anyone else in this room, a product of heredity and environment. If you take away my body and all my memories of a life away from me, what remains is not I.

Princess : But does anything remain, Prince?

P. Chanakaya : I do not know. The matter cannot be settled one way or the other. But if anything were to remain, it would not be me.

Princess : Something can remain, something imperishable, you grant the possibility, yet you say it is not you.

P. Chanakaya : Your Highness, *if* anything remains, which is only a possibility, a good possibility I admit, that something is part of the universal self, which is not specifically me.

Princess : And therefore...

P. Chanakaya : And therefore when I die, I die. If my soul goes into another body, a new born baby's body, be it man or animal, it does not truly count as an afterlife, because where is my own individual continuity.

Princess : But Prince, there are instances of people remembering their past lives.

P. Chanakaya : I grant we have some cases, and some of them appear to be authentic too. Others may just be fantasies. Even it is true, my point is that there is no continuity. Those persons were different, molded under the circumstances of a different age, received a different education, had completely different parents, wives, children, had a different personality, *where* is the continuity? When we speak of an afterlife, we always imply some kind of continuity. No, there is no afterlife, in this earth or on any planet called Heaven.

Princess : What is your point, Chanakaya? I am a bit confused.

P. Chanakaya : Your Highness, I accept what Socrates says that the life force itself may be indestructible...

Princess : (interrupting) And what of the soul?

P. Chanakaya : It is the same thing I refer to, Your Highness. The life force, or the soul, call it what you will. The soul, certainly, if it exists, is a kind of life force.

Princess : So you are saying...

P. Chanakaya : That the soul and the life force may be indestructible, but there is no continuity maintained, so the notion of an afterlife is irrelevant. It is metamorphosis, without continuity.

Princess : Your talk is most interesting, Chanakaya. However could there not be continuity in these metamorphoses ...

P. Chanakaya : In the absence of memory, what kind of continuity could there be?

It's reinventing the wheel- in a different form.

Princess : What do you mean?

P. Chanakaya : Your Highness, take our colonies. In their primitive religion, what we deem primitive, they have a notion of heaven and hell.

Princess : Yes, they do.

P. Chanakaya : They also believe in an afterlife. They

believe that after death, the person goes to heaven or to hell, depending on his moral conduct during the course of his life.

Princess : Yes, go on.

P. Chanakaya : We Bharatians ridicule this idea and dismiss it as primitive. The notion of two planets circling around, one with all kinds of comforts and the other with all kinds of tortures is too childish to convince anyone with some little intelligence. No offence to you, Prince Socrates.

P. Socrates : None taken, Prince. I am in perfect agreement with you, on the absurdity of our theological understanding.

P. Chanakaya : (turns back to the Princess) When you propose this continuity in metamorphosis, are you not perhaps suggesting that the continuity is based on some kind of a moral vision, which permeates the entire universe?

Princess : I admit it is so, Prince.

P. Chanakaya : So you reinvent the idea of heaven and hell, or reward and punishment according to one's moral behavior, but in a much more sophisticated form, do you not?

Princess : That's true.

P. Chanakaya : If we commit good deeds in this life, we are rewarded in the next life by being born as a Prince or Princess. On the other hand if we lead a sinful life, we shall be reborn as a leper or maybe as a dirty animal.

Princess : That could be a possibility, could it not?

P. Chanakaya : If this were true, it would still not be a moral universe.

Princess : Why not?

P. Chanakaya : Because the Prince who was born as a

prince because of his virtuous conduct in a past life would commit all kinds of sins in the present one, and then go back to what he was. There is no continuous evolvement...

Princess : And why do you suppose not?

P. Chanakaya : Because, Princess, we live in eternity.

Princess : (thoughtfully) But then everything would be without purpose. Without meaning.

P. Chanakaya : Perhaps the universe is already perfect.

Princess : (smiles) Perhaps. Well... excuse me gentlemen. Please enjoy your *sherbet.*

The Princess goes back to sit on her throne next to her great-uncle Sanjay.

Sanjay : (whispers loudly) Have you decided then, my Princess?

Princess : No, it's too difficult. Maybe I should short list.

Sanjay : This is *already* a short list, my dear child. Proposals originally came in from at least a hundred princes and there are only nine seated here. You can't *keep* short listing . . . and add to the anxiety of these young princes.

Princess : Well, all of them do not appear to be so young. Besides, it **is** difficult. I'll tell you what the problem is. (whispers in his ear)

Sanjay : What?! The white prince too. Don't do this, my dear, I beg of you.

Princess : No, *Chacha*, these are the two. I have decided.

Sanjay : (wearily)Well, I hope you know what you're doing my dear. (beckons a elderly maid standing near to the princess) Anidabai, come here.

On being thus summoned, the maid approaches, curtsies.

Sanjay : Listen very carefully, Anidabai. Take this rose - it is our national flower, isn't it? - and stick it into the button hole of that gentleman wearing the blue *achkan*. (points at Socrates) Have you understood?

Anidabai : Yes, sire.

Sanjay : Wait, don't go away. I haven't finished as yet. There is one *more* rose. (picks up another flower) and that is to be placed in the button hole of that gentleman wearing that black *bandgala.* (points at Chanakaya)

Anidabai : (startled) Two roses, sire?!

Sanjay : (impatiently) Yes, yes! Didn't you hear me?! The Princess had determined that it will be one of those two gentlemen who will have the good fortune. Go now and do as I have bidden.

(The maid curtseys to the Princess and Sanjay, then withdraws and does as she has been instructed. The Princes seated at the tables are all suddenly very tense, aware that the time of reckoning has come. Prince Chanakaya can be seen to be holding the edges of the table with his hands, when the maid first approaches Prince Socrates seated on an adjoining table, and affixes the rose onto his buttonhole. He relaxes however, when she comes and puts a rose in his buttonhole as well. The tension is released. The other princes look disappointed particularly Prince Veerappa, but it is clear to all of them, as the royal maid goes back to sit (stand) in a corner, that only two of the suitors have been thus favored. Gradually, as is the custom in such royal *swayamvaras*, one by one all the rejected Princes leave the hall, leaving only two, our heroes, Chanakaya and Socrates.)

Sanjay : (stands up and approaches Princes Chanakaya and Socrates) Gentlemen!! The Princess has made her decision. It will be the one or the other. The matter will be settled by contest. (sees their expression) No, not any physical contest. You know our princess is of too delicate a temperament to enjoy any display of brute physical prowess. It will be a test of your intelligence and knowledge.

Chanakaya : Yes, sire. Pray where and when is this contest to take place?

Sanjay : It will be at noon tomorrow, an auspicious time of day. At noon tomorrow will be decided the question of who has succeeded in conquering our princess's heart. Unlike today's ceremony, which has been totally private in the interests of decorum, important dignitaries of State including cabinet ranking ministers will view the contest. Fare thee well both till then.

Socrates : (bows)And the same to you and the Princess.

Chanakaya : . . . and the Princess (bows).

Exit Socrates And Chanakaya

Sanjay : So, we are left alone.

Princess : Who do you think is better, *chacha*?

Sanjay : Most definitely Prince Chanakaya. (pauses) And my dear, it *must* be Chanakaya. People are going to be most upset with any other result.

Princess : Oh, come now, *chacha,* you know I will not do anything foolish.

Sanjay : I sincerely hope you won't my child.Go and rest now, Princess. You must be tired with all this excitement.

Princess : No, I'm not tired. It was all very interesting. You know, *chachu*, father came to me in a dream last night.

Sanjay : That's understandable my dear that he should be thinking of you at the time of your marriage.

Princess : It seemed to me that he was trying to tell

me something.

Sanjay : Perhaps he was trying to warn you against including Prince Socrates in the *swayamvara* short list.

Princess : No, no, *chacha*. Some things I did hear him say. He told me of how he was ashamed of some of his actions against the people of Blighty.

Sanjay : That must have been the infamous sterilization campaign, and the massacre at Tundun he alluded to.

Princess : Yes, yes. That was it, I think. He was about to give me some advice when I suddenly woke up. Oh, I wish I knew what he was going to say. Can you tell me a little about that time?

Sanjay : You sure you don't want to read a copy of V. Almiki's 'History of Maha Bharat.'

Princess : No, *chacha,* I don't want merely to read. I want to see. And we know you have been gifted with the power to see. And to make others see. Tonight, I want you to make me see.

Sanjay : (thoughtfully) I see. (pauses as if thinking) Well, all right, I'll show you three scenes from the past. The Round Table Conference, the infamous sterilization campaign carried out by General Brandy and Col. Mossambi . . . and we can end with some erotic stuff, considering you're of age now

Curtain Falls

Scene 6

The stage gradually lightens to show a large, round conference table on which are seated Jahanpanah (JP), Prime Minister Behru, General Brandy, Colonel Mossambi and a Scientist. When the curtain lifts it is still dark, there are some flashes of lightning then, rumbles of a thunder like sound and an explosion. A voice in the background (it is Sanjay's voice) is speaking in a darkened stage.

Voice : It is the year 1935, the year in which the jewel in the crown of the Empire of Maha Bharat nearly slipped out. The year that foretold of the eventual break up and complete disintegration of the Bharatian Empire. A round table conference is taking place at Indraprastha, the capital of Maha Bharat.

Behru : Your Highness, these days there are many editorials in the newspapers of Blighty which suggest that the Blitz should be given independence.

JP : (snorts at the suggestion is disapproval) These journalists talk such nonsense, and sometimes our Bhartian scribes are actually worse than the Blitz ones. I wonder you give their views any importance, Prime Minister.

Behru : (defensively) It's not only the scribes, Your Highness. I believe that they are emboldened in expressing their opinion, which they have never dared to do earlier, because of the ferment at the ground level. The whole of Blighty is in turmoil. Students have decided not to go to University, schools are shut, the Blitz lawyers are boycotting the Courts, and now most recently and worryingly even upper-class Blitz housewives who have always collaborated with us earlier, have given up their knitting and evening tea parties, and instead come out to participate in rallies and demonstrations against the imperial Bharatian empire. Why, in some of these public gatherings Blitz men and women make speeches and start bonfires where shirts, skirts and blouses manufactured in Bharatian factories in Vernice[17] and Monacca[18] are set ablaze. Terrorists in some of our other territories are supporting these Blitz patriots in their efforts as well. It appears that the entire white race is up in arms.

JP : Hmmn. What you say is disturbing, Prime Minister. Very disturbing indeed. However . . . simply no question of giving them independence or self-rule or whatever else they are hankering for. What do you say, General Brandy?

G. Brand : Never, sire. They'll start killing each other the minute we leave. They be like chillun, my king.

JP : Exactly! Blighty is a land of children. They are a child race, stunted, and dwarfed . . . Mr Behru?

Behru : As I said there is a fair amount of unrest there. They wish to be able to elect their own king.

JP : Elect a king! That's a contradiction in terms. What nonsense!! What will they come up with next? (thinks) General, can you not quell these disturbance? If things go on at this rate, it may stir up matters in our other dominions as well. Those people have been under control till now, but who knows? They may start getting ideas as well.

17. For Varanasi
18. Dacca muslin was famous

Behru : (quietly) Birchbill is quoted in the papers today as saying that not all the armies in the world can stop an idea whose time has come.

JP : What nonsense!! Must be some foolish Blitz. As if ideas have a life of their own!! This sounds a bit like their Holy Ghost nonsense. I think you are reading the wrong books these days, prime minister. General, what do you have to say?

G. Brandy : (eagerly) With your permission, sir, I wish to propose . . . .

C. Mossambi : (who has been silent till now but now wishes to make his presence felt) The basic problem, sire, which I suggested to the General, is that their numbers is growing too fastly. Them white people be breeding like rabbits, sire.

G. Brandy : Col. Mossambi, please be quiet . . . and don't interrupt me again (glares at him) (turns to JP) As I was saying, Your Highness, the major historical advantages we have had over the Blitz is of belonging to a vastly superior civilization with more developed weaponry. To these advantages has been added the advantage of numbers. The small armies of their local kings were too small to be any match for our huge ground and naval forces. For a few decades now as the Colonel indicates, the Blitz are breeding like rabbits.

JP : (impatiently) Well, nothing can be done about that . . . or can it? (a puzzled expression appears on his face) General . . . are you suggesting we can do something about *that*?! What on earth *can* you do, short of putting the entire population into prisons? As it is our jails are overcrowded. We have had to pack off terrorists from the Blitz Kreig to islands like Black Water[19]. But Black Water is no

19. Kala Pani

solution for a problem like this.

G. Brandy : (all eagerness now) Your Highness, there **is** a way. I have discovered one . . . with the help of Col. Mossambi and Mr Scientist.

JP : What's this, Mr. Scientist? Some new invention from the laboratory? A medicine, a pill that we get the Blitz ladies to swallow - and then they cannot conceive. Is that it? We've been hearing of such an invention for decades. (It'll be useful for us as well)

Scientist : I'm afraid, Your Highness, that we haven't been able to invent something like that as yet. But we will. Assuredly, we will. The problem, Highness, is that our initial investigations have shown us that such a pill when it is finally developed will be effective only for a limited period of time. On their own the ladies may decide not to take the pill. We would have to ask the ladies to keep coming every fortnight to ensure that they take the medicine. We've found a better solution that will solve the problem once for all.

JP : (yawning) Mr Scientist, please don't bore me with these technical details. Come to the point. What is it?

Scientist : Your Highness, there has been an unprecedented advance in certain surgical techniques. A simple ten-minute operation has to be performed on the men . . . and that's it. If Your Highness . . .

Behru : (agitated) Forgive me for interrupting, Mr Scientist, but is this operation you speak of - this *sterilization,* I suppose one must call it - perfectly *safe.*

Scientist : To be honest, Prime Minister, we need to refine the surgical equipment and technique somewhat before it is so . . . but we are nearly there.

G. Brandy : If Your Highness will please give me the permission . . .

Behru : I don't think we should be so hasty, General.

JP : On the other hand, let's not be too squeamish, Prime Minister. Yes, you have my permission, General. Do whatever you feel is necessary. Yet, remember, if things should go wrong, I shall have your heads. Yours and Col. Mossambi's. Now make plans to leave for Blighty at once.

G. Brandy : Please, Your Highness.

JP : And keep me posted of developments. I shall expect a telegraphic update from you every week.

G. Brandy : Please, Your Highness. Can we then take your leave, Your Highness?

JP : Yes, you may go.

Exit General Brandy, Col. Mossambi and the Scientist

Behru : With due respect, my King, I believe you have acted in haste.

JP : Forget that. Tell me, Behru, is it true that you are a friend of Mrs Birchbill.

Behru : Well, yes. I suppose so. As much as I am of Mr Birchbill himself.

JP : Oh, forget that old fool. Why don't you then tell Mrs Birchbill that she should use her powers to persuade Mr Birchbill to call off his agitation, and we will make sure he is adequately rewarded for it? Haven't the supporters of our imperial presence in that land done well for themselves? Like that lawyer, the elder Pearlson.

Behru : I don't think, Your Highness, that Ms Birchbill would exercise the kind of influence you speak of on a man like Birchbill. He's like a rock, the man is.

JP : (disappointed) Well, no harm done if you try.

Behru : With all respect, Your Highness, I don't think I could bring myself to even try, so certain am I that such a move could have only negative consequences for us.

JP : I think that having been bereaved early in your marriage, you tend to underestimate the power of wives, Prime Minister.

Behru : Besides, Highness, to be perfectly honest, I actually believe that the world is a changed place now, and it would now actually be far better for us if we did give the Linglish people limited self-rule.

JP : (snorts contemptuously) Self-rule! You're completely deluded, Prime Minister. They're not ready for that as yet. They'd be at each other's throats in no time. The General is right. The Blitz, the Bots, the Squelsh and that perennial foe of the Blitz, the Virishman. They will simply butcher each other if we aren't there to stop them.

Behru : (primly) I beg to differ, Your Highness.

JP : Differ away. You know I have never minded difference of opinion and have always considered it to be a sign of a healthy polity, like my ancestor Emperor Akbar. Do you know, Prime Minister, the reason why in the famous mutiny of 1857, the people of Blighty lost to us?

Behru : There were a number of reasons.

JP : The *single* most important factor. I'm talking about that. More important than civilizational superiority. More important than an advantage in numbers, or superior weaponry. (speaks with emphasis now) It was that we were united and have been so since the time of my great ancestor, Emperor Akbar. The Blitz people were NOT. Even the peoples of such a small island couldn't stay together in peace. The Bots, the Virish, the Welshy, they all thought of themselves as different from and indeed superior to the others. They *hated* the Blitz. The people of Blighty hated them. And we, we were able to take advantage of their disunity, crush the rebellion and deliver a lasting blow to the movement. The Virish - they were on our side, weren't they? Fought together side by side with the Bharatian troops. Brave people, the Virish. And trustworthy too. Not like the Blitz, they are slimier. Well . . . the point I am making, which must be already clear to you, is that these white people are like children, truant children, not well behaved ones, mind you. They cannot as yet, be trusted to take care of themselves. If we give them limited self-rule today, in a few months they will ask for complete independence. They cannot as yet be trusted to take care of themselves. It's not good for them, I tell you. For their *own* good, we must not give them freedom, damn it.

Behru : As I said earlier, the natives are getting restless . . . and their leader Mr Birchbill has vowed that he will not rest till they are free. There is also the case of Mr Pearlson's son, the militant revolutionary. He's acquiring quite a following too.

JP : Well, as far as Mr Birchbill is concerned, you know basically he's quite sensible . . . but the younger Pearlson is bonkers. The trouble with Birchbill is that he's so self-righteous. Some of these Blitz leaders can be so self-righteous and pompous. (laughs) They almost act as if they were ruling *us* instead of the other way around. (thinks for a while) The situation requires very careful handling. I'm not sure if General Brandy and Col. Mossambi are up to it. Although the idea of sterilization is excellent, they might make some stupid mistakes in the implementation. I tell you what, Behru. Pack your bags and go off to Tundun by the next ship. Form your own independent assessment of the situation and don't rely anymore on newspaper reports, as you appear to have been doing. Newspaper reports are not reliable, I tell you. I will be relieved that you are there to keep an eye on General Brandy and Col. Mossambi.

Behru : As Your Highness wishes.

JP : I shall wait for your full report, which you must telegraph me at the earliest. (thinks for a while) Tell you what, Behru. Just to show you that I actually have an open mind on the question of granting them limited self-governance, in a week's time I'll send off an invitation to Mr Birchbill to come to Maha Bharat for a Round Table Conference on the question. While the conference is underway, I will have the advantage of your full report and will know how best to handle him.

Behru : Why, that's an excellent idea, my King!

JP : (leeringly) With him out of the way, it'll also give you a free hand with his wife.

Behru : (blushes, but ignores the King's comment) I'll prepare to leave then, Your Highness.

Curtain

Scene 7

A week later. The drawing room of Birchbill's home at St Mary's in the Southwest of Blighty. This town forms part of the Isles of Scilly, an archipelago of five inhabited islands and numerous other rocky islets. It is the seat of the Bharatian Empire's winter capital. Birchbill is with his wife Clementine. They are having tea.

Clementine : How was Tundun, my dear?

Birchbill : Cold. Bloody cold. It's nice and warm here at St Mary's by comparison.

Clementine : It's the best place to be in the winter, my dear.

Birchbill : You know, one has to hand this to the Bhartians. What were the Isles of Scilly before they came and developed them? Rocky, abandoned places nobody ever visited. Now you find nice paved roads and beautiful buildings everywhere. Gardens, beaches!!

Clementine : Well, you know the Bhartians needed to feel warm, as our winter is very severe.

Birchbill : *I* also need to feel warm. They *did* it. Linked up these desolate islands with the mainland with a remarkable transport system. Today, all the rich people of Tundun flock to St Mary's in the winter.

Clementine : You're quite right, my dear. I suppose we do have to give credit to the Bharatians for all this.

Birchbill : (ruefully) I suppose I'm going to be still

warmer when I sail up to Kayrashi next week and then go up to Indraprastha in the North.

Clementine : Do you *have* to go, Birchy?

Birchbill : (irritably) Yes, of course I have to go. The Jahanpanah has sent a wire inviting me to be present at the Round Table Conference to be held at Indraprastha next month. Anyway, I don't quite understand what you're making such a fuss about, woman. You have enough to amuse yourself with.

Clementine : Only tea parties and gossip with the ladies, Birchy. That wouldn't compensate for your absence. I'll miss you.

Birchbill : Confound it, woman. Act naturally, for God's sake. (suspiciously) Is there something you want from me?

Clementine : (hesitating) Well, husband . . . I thought we could do it today.

Birchbill : Control yourself, woman. Don't start behaving like your mother! (bites his tongue) Oh, dear, I'm sorry. I didn't mean to say that.

Clementine : (in tears) Of course you meant to! Always shaming me with my illegitimacy. As if *your* mother was very virtuous.

Birchbill : No, she wasn't. She was even worse than yours. I'll grant that. Well, then, stop behaving like *my* mother.

Clementine : It's only because you're leaving and I won't see you for two months that I thought we could do it just this once.

Birchbill : (in a conciliatory tone) Well, we can't . Don't make it difficult for me, dear. You have to support me in this. Try and look more cheerful. I won't be gone long. (puts his arms around her)

Clementine : (somewhat soothed, gains control over her feelings) I'm sorry, my dear. I know you've taken a vow. I just couldn't help myself today.

Birchbill : I'm sorry, my dear, but you know how it is. Celibacy vows are not to be trifled with. You know I have sworn never to touch meat or woman till I win my country's independence.

Clementine : (changing the topic) Do you think, Birchy dear, that the Jahanpanah really means to grant us self-rule?

Birchbill : (thoughtful for a few moments) I'm not sure. To tell you the truth, I was greatly surprised by the telegram. I wasn't expecting it at all. Of course it may prove to be quite insincere. He may just want me away from Blighty, and Tundun in particular, at this time when everything is in such ferment.

Clementine : Well, then, if he's just playing a game, need you go?

Birchbill : I don't think there is any choice, but that I have to go, *even* if he's playing a game.

Clementine : What will you wear when you go to see the Jahanpanah?

Birchbill : (angrily) What will I wear? I don't understand you woman. I will wear what I have always worn. The traditional Blitz dress.

Clementine : But the climate in Maha Bharat will be so very warm. Perhaps you should wear a light *kurta* with a *churidaar pajama*. These Bharatian clothes are so practical for the summer.

Birchbill : Bharatian clothes! Have you gone mad, Clementine? What an outrageous suggestion! Why, what will the peasantry in the villages of Blighty say to that! Do not underestimate the value of symbols, my dear.

Clementine : At least then the newspapers won't publish those nasty remarks about your dress, that they did the last time.

Birchbill : You mean (quotes): 'Overdressed buffoon striding up the steps of the *Diwan-i- Khas* to come and parley with the Jahanpanah on equal terms.' Let such things be said, my dear. Barking dogs never bite. It does not matter. They will not deter me from my resolve.

Clementine : I'm sure the Bhartian media is bound to be impressed by your steely determination. But that foolish Jahanpanah. I'm told he simply doesn't care what the newspapers print.

Birchbill : At his own peril, my dear.

Clementine : I'm sure if it had been in Mr Behru's powers, we would have had self-rule by now.

Birchbill : (enthusiastically) Now there's a man you can't help but admire, even though he's on the opposite camp. Someone who sees the whole pointlessness of war and violence.

Clementine : Mr Behru is so dignified and charming. All the ladies in Blighty simply adore him.

Birchbill : Well, make him comfortable if he comes to Blighty while I'm away. There's a very good chance our ships may cross each other on the ocean. My informers at the Indraprastha Palace have told me that General Brandy, Col. Mosambi and Behru are all three on their way to Tundun. That's the other odd thing about the timing of Jahanpanah's telegram. One would have thought that he would want an experienced hand like Behru next to him while negotiations for self-rule were taking place. Instead, he sends him to Tundun.

Clementine : (wisely) Perhaps he wants to make sure that the General and the Colonel don't get up to too much mischief. Behru's presence will act as a restraining influence on them.

Birchbill : (rubbing his chin) Yes, that's possible. Perfectly possible. Besides, while Jahanpanah allows himself to be influenced to an extent by jokers like that General Brandy and Colonel Mossambi, it's Behru's advice he really relies on. (snaps his fingers) Maybe, that's it! He wants Behru to make an assessment of the situation in Tundun. The mood of the people and so on. The Round Table Conference will proceed according to the wireless reports Behru sends him from here.

Clementine : Oh, I'm sure Mr Behru will send him favorable reports. I mean reports favorable to our cause.

Birchbill : Don't be so sure, woman. I know that Behru is internally convinced of the justness of our demand for self-rule, but don't forget he's a great patriot and loyal to the king. If he feels the Imperial Government of Maha Bharat can pull along for another few years without much trouble, he will say so to the King, despite being internally quite sympathetic to our cause.

Clementine : (suddenly looking quite cheerful) He's such a dear, isn't he?

Birchbill : If Mr Behru comes down to St Mary's from Tundun, do invite him for a meal.(a thought seems to strike him) By the way, be very careful of one thing while Behru is around.

Clementine : (somewhat startled) What about? He's a gentleman.

Birchbill : (impatiently) I know that!! I meant that you should say nothing that may make him feel that the situation can be dragged on for some time.

Clementine : (very sweetly) Don't worry, my dearest. We'll keep him amused by other devices. Shan't talk politics at all.

Birchbill : Mind you don't. Yet make his trip as pleasurable as you can. Well, I guess I'd better be going now. It's time for my ship. (the bell rings) That must be the coachman.

Clementine : Goodbye, my dear.

Birchbill : Goodbye Clementine. (gives her a peck on the cheek) I'm glad to see you looking cheerful finally . . . and I'm sorry for all the nasty things I said.

Clementine : Don't distress yourself on my account, Birchbill. The needs of the country are certainly greater than that of a woman. Please take care of yourself. The nation, more than I needs you.

Birchbill : History shall remember your contribution, Clementine.

Curtain

Scene 8

The drawing room of Lord Pearlson's house in Central Tundun. Lord Pearlson and his son Ruby are in the middle of an argument. It is evening time.

Pearlson : If I don't object to the clothes you wear, son, I don't see why you, or anyone else for that matter, should object to what I'm wearing.

Ruby : It's shameful! That's why I object.

Pearlson : Listen, kiddo. You may be the newest happening on the block, but I'm still *your* father, and not the other way around. Don't try and act as if you were *my* father.

Ruby : (looking sorrowful) Why can't you try and understand?! All my friends laugh at you, and I have to perforce join in their laughter. It's so embarrassing to have a father like you.

Pearlson : And all my friends and colleagues at the Bar sneer at me for having a son like you. Someone who has had the good fortune to have the best of education, studied at the Institutes of Higher Learning at Indraprastha, and Saraswati - how many children have such an opportunity? - but who insists on dressing up like a tramp. What, by the way, do *your* friends have to say about the state of my attire? It would interest me to know whether they feel their own dress is more stylish, or even comfortable.

Ruby : (losing all patience) They say that you dress up just like a White Sahib. The White Sa'ab's who imitate their brown masters in everything they eat, drink or wear.

Pearlson : So what's wrong with dressing up like the brownies. It's better by any objective, fair standard.

Ruby : People say your *churidaars* are tailored at Indraprastha and sent to Tundun by ship at great expense.

Pearlson : It is the truth. If they so you, they say so with admiration.

Ruby : It is only the foolish and the ignorant who admire such things.

Pearlson : And my medals - do they not speak of them as well. (goes up to a mantelpiece where various decorations and ribbon-wrapped certificates are placed, picks up a medal and caresses it lovingly) And this OBE. Order of the Blue Peacock. More highly prized than even the ORS, Order of the Rising Sun. Most of my colleagues would give their eyeteeth to possess this in their own merit. Do they not regard it highly, your friends?

Ruby : (scornfully) They regard it with the contempt it deserves. It is owing to people like you that our independence has been delayed by so many years.

Pearlson : Listen, son, it will not happen in my lifetime, nor in yours. Do you know how large the Empire is? It used to be said in the days of my youth that the moon always shines on the Bharatian Empire. Somewhere on the globe, at this very time while we sit (stand) here talking, it is night and the moon is shining, and casting a glow over what forms part of their territory. The Bharatians outnumber us by far. They are hundreds of millions of them and we are so few. In recent years it is true that our population has been growing rapidly, but that is part of the problem, not the solution. It will only aggravate the terrible living conditions of our populace. Do you seriously consider that a small island like us can resist the mighty forces of the Bharatian army?

Ruby : (determinedly) We will do it one day soon, father.

Pearlson : After Blighty they conquered the great continent to our east, then the two great continents to our west and finally the continent to our south. Empire builders!! Truly great men, were they not?!

Ruby : You shame me, father. I despise myself for having been born in such a household.

Enter Footman

Footman : (addressing L. Pearlson) Sire, there is someone who wants to meet Master Ruby.

Ruby : Let him in. It must be John. He said he would drop by with the latest news.

Pearlson : I'm afraid, my son, you cannot anymore call your militant friends from Blitz Krieg to this house. It will put me in the bad books of the government.

Ruby : I don't suppose I should continue to stay here either in that case. If my friends are not welcome . . .

Pearlson : Not until and unless you mend your ways. At least with Mr Birchbill, one knows that one is dealing with a pacifist, but some of your friends, I believe, are nothing short of criminals. Let this be the last visit from one of your political friends.

Enter John

John : (visibly excited, but blanches at the sight of Lord Pearlson) Ruby, I came to ask if you are coming.

Ruby : What's up, John?

John : That Bharatian monster, General Brandy and his henchman Col. Mossambi are busy performing vasectomies on innocent poor people.

Ruby : Vasectomy? What's that?

John : It's the newly coined medical term for an operation in which they cut up a tube in your penis so that you cannot produce any children. It's a conspiracy to undermine our manhood and our struggles. Besides the operation isn't safe as yet. The medical tools are crude.

Pearlson : (aggressively) How do you know? How do you know the operation isn't safe? Have you been operated upon?

John : No, but it's not safe, uncle, believe me. A number of persons have died at the operating table.

Ruby : Where are these . . . these operations being carried out?

John : Right next to old fort near the river Thames. They've cordoned off a huge area and set up a make shift camp of sorts. A huge crowd has gathered outside to protest these forcible sterilizations. That's where I'm heading. Are you coming, Ruby?

Ruby : Yes, of course.

Pearlson : I absolutely forbid you to go, my son. You must not go. The Bharatians are absolutely right. We are too many in numbers and it is for our own good that these operations are being carried out. That is why we are such a poor country.

(Make the situation such - mention it in the earlier scene of the Round Table - that the Bharatian population though higher than the Blitz population actually remained stable whereas the Blitz pop has been growing by leaps and bounds)

Ruby : Father, you quite shame me. I do not think I shall return to this house after all.

Pearlson : Wait, son, wait. It's not quite safe for you to go there today . . . and John, you must also desist. This matter came up in the morning in the High Court on a petition filed on behalf of some nationalist Blitz organization. The Bharatian Judge who heard arguments has dismissed the case. According to the order passed by him the operations - these sterilizations - are perfectly legal, being carried out in the public interest to help rid the Blitz people of a life of poverty and penury.

Ruby : What utter nonsense!

John : We don't be accepting the verdict of such a Court.

Ruby : A kangaroo Court, that's what it is.

Pearlson : (greatly agitated now) Wait, son, wait. You haven't heard the whole story. On a specific plea regarding the use of force, His Lordship has ruled that the Bharatian army could be deployed by the administration to remove and disperse any unlawful obstruction to the medical operations . . . and if necessary may even open fire! And I have it on good authority that that's precisely what they intend to do today itself.

Ruby : (looking sorrowful) And you did not tell me even this. Adieu, father. Goodbye.

John : (excited) It's unprecedented! How can they do this!

Ruby : *Chalo*, John. Let's go comrade.

Curtain

Scene 9

The Stage is in Darkness

Voice in the Background (Sanjay) : Princess, you are about to witness the famous scene of the Tundun massacre which took place inside an old fort besides the river Thames. You wanted to know how the White man was persecuted and treated worse than an animal by us, didn't you Princess? Here, see it for yourself. This is how it all happened. Right now the infamous sterilizations are taking place under the personal supervision of General Brandy and Col. Mossambi. A surgeon[20] is busy performing the operation, that is to say he is hacking away at the private parts of the White prisoners. He is assisted by an attractive looking nurse[21]. As you will see, the sterilization technique, which has become sophisticated nowadays, was rather crude in those times.

The Stage Lightens

Inside a fortress like structure are assembled the Bhartian Special Forces dressed in military gear. It is a *kurta-pajama* uniform they are wearing, possibly a brownish *kurta* and white pajamas (*churidaars*). There are several White prisoners in chains; looking unwashed, unshaved and they are dressed mostly in rags. There is a *khaki* colored tent inside the fortress and a chained queue of prisoners is waiting outside the entrance. The maroon *kurta*ed sentries are forcing the prisoners inside with the use of sticks and rods and these men are then shortly afterwards emerging from the other side of the tent groaning in

20. The Scientist in a double role
21. Lady Mohabattein in a double role

pain. General Brandy is busy overseeing and directing most of the proceedings. Prisoners who survive the operation are allowed to go. Others die. Colonel Mossambi directs the dead bodies to be kept aside in a corner and they are piling up. Sentries are on guard positioned outside the main gate to the fortress.

G. Brandy : Get into the tent, you bloody fool! Don't you understand plain Prustian? Shall I speak to you in Bhindi then?

Prisoner : No, no . . . . Please! I got a wife and kids.

G. Brandy : That's why you need to get in, gow. You got too many kids already. This will make sure you can't have any more.

Prisoner : Please let me go, sir. I beg of you!!

G. Brandy : (wielding the stick, hits the man twice) GO IN, I said! Bloody gow!

The man enters the tent, where the Surgeon is awaiting him. (dressed in white, a white cloth over his face) There is a bed in which the patient is expected to lie down. The nurse is there to help him.

Surgeon : Come in my man, come in. Don't look so scared. Are you a woman or a man!!

Prisoner : Sir, please, I beg of you . . . .

Surgeon : I don't want any of your nonsense, gow. We have to perform two hundred operations today, that's the target. Now, don't waste my time. Just take off your trousers and lie low on the bed. Pronto!!

Prisoner : Take off my trousers! No!!

Surgeon : You better do as I say my friend, or you'll be the worse for it. (leeringly) Or do you want our pretty nurse here to help you take them off? (sternly) Take them off, I said! Here, take this sheet, you can cover yourself with it.

(His instructions having been complied with, the surgeon begins the operation)

Surgeon : Pass me the scissors, nurse.

Nurse : Here, sir.

Surgeon : Now the scalpel.

Nurse : Here, sir.

Surgeon : Now pass me the string. I need to tie up the tubes.

Nurse : Here, sir, here is some string.

Surgeon : (takes it from her) Thanks. (He is busy for a minute.) Nurse!

Nurse : Yes, sir.

Surgeon : Now pass me the cello- tape.

Nurs : We've run out of cello-tape, sir.

Surgeon : Hell! What are we going to do? We need the cello-tape otherwise everything will just hang loose.

Nurse : Shall I give you a rubber, sir?

Surgeon : (shocked) A rubber!

Nurse : (sweetly) A rubber band, sir. I've got plenty of those.

Surgeon : Oh! That's an excellent idea. Yes, give me one of those. That should hold everything together.

Nurse : One rubber band coming up.

Surgeon : There! The whole thing is finished. You may go now, my man.

Patient : (disbelievingly) Can I really go?

Surgeon : Yes, of course. There are so many other patients waiting. We don't want to try their patience. (shouts) Next!

The patient staggers to the outside of the tent and collapses. Col Mossambi is waiting outside the tent with two helpers.

C. Mossambi : This one's copped it too, 'asnt he?

First Helper : Yes, sir. (feels his pulse) Perfectly dead, sir.

C. Mossambi : He was all right when he came out, wasn't he?

Second Helper : That's right, sir. Let me see. (peers closely at the patient who is lying prostrate) I think that's what's done it!

C. Mossambi : What?

Second Helper : The rubber band, sir. It's snapped.

C. Mossambi : I see! Well, then, if he's dead, put his body with the rest of the corpses.

The two attendants do as they have been instructed. Meanwhile, the family members of those who are being operated upon (or of those who have died) have gathered outside the fortress, together with white bermuda clad members of the Blitz Kreig[22].

First Man : Where is Comrade John, for Chrissake?

Second Man : He's gone to get Ruby.

First Man : They should have been here by now.

Second Man : What shall we do?

First Man : There! They are both coming.

Comrades John and Ruby arrive to join the gathering.

Ruby : So this is what is happening!

John : What should we do, Comrade Ruby?

Ruby : For starters, let's start shouting in protest. Ready, comrades.

Chorus : Ready!!

Ruby : (loudly) Bharatian Government.

Chorus : Down, down.

John : Blitz Kreig

Chorus : Up, up.

22. The white Bermudas could be replaced by other appropriate gear. The Rashtriya Swayam Sevak's in India are known to wear khaki shorts.

Ruby : General Brandy

Chorus : Shame, shame.

(It is repeated once more)

Ruby : Bharatian Government

Chorus : Down, down.

John : Blitz Kreig

Chorus : Up, up

Ruby : General Brandy

Chorus : Shame, shame

(The shouting reaches General Brandy's ears.)

G. Brandy : (shouts) Colonel Mossambi.

C. Mossambi : (marches forward and salutes) Yes, sir!

G. Brandy : At ease. Colonel, can you hear that racket? What the devil is going on?

C. Mossambi : I'm not quite sure, sir.

G. Brandy : Just go and check up, will you? All this shouting is giving me a headache. Just get them to quieten down, will you?

C. Mossambi : Yes, sir. At once.

(Colonel Mossambi goes up to the Gate and starts conferring with the sentries posted there, who are watching the protesters shout.)

Ruby : (spotting the Colonel, raises a fresh cry) Col. Mossambi!!

Chorus : Shame, shame!

Ruby : Governmental ass!

Chorus : Down, down!!

C. Mossambi : Hey, you!

Ruby : (innocently) You addressing me, mister.

C. Mossambi : Yes, I'm speaking to you. Keep quiet, will you? The General doesn't like to be disturbed in his afternoon nap.

Ruby : (once more taking up the cry) Col. Mossambi!

Chorus : Shame, shame!!

C. Mossambi : (wagging his finger angrily) All right then. I'll go and tell the General. You know how brutal he can be. He'll fix the lot of you.

John : General Brandy!!

Chorus : Shame, shame!!

C. Mossambi : (reporting to the General) Sir, these people refuse to keep quiet. Shall I order a *lathi* charge, sir, to get them to disperse.

G. Brandy : No, no that will be too long and messy. Besides the injured ones will then still be there, screaming their heads off. I'm not in the mood for that kind of music today. Sometimes I do enjoy it, Colonel Mossambi, but not today.

C. Mossambi : (sympathetically) I understand, sir.

G. Brandy : I have this terrible headache, you see . . .

C. Mossambi : (even more sympathetic) I understand perfectly, sir. Shall I then just order them to be all shot, sir?

G. Brandy : (thinks for a moment) No, let's not be hasty. We must give them one chance. As the Blitz Bard says the spirit of justice must be tempered by mercy. Wait, I'll come with you . . . and have this whole thing settled one way or the other.

G. Brandy and C. Mossambi come up to the gate

G. Brandy : (loudly) What's happening here, my friends? Why are you disturbing the peace?

(The shouting dies down. The crowd falls silent. There is murmuring. 'General Brandy,' they whisper to each other.)

Ruby : (passionately) It is not us, General, but you

who are disturbing the peace.

G. Brandy : (very cool) Oh, I see. An angry young man. We know how to deal with angry young men, Colonel Mossambi, don't we?

C. Mossambi : Yes, sir, indeed we do!!

G. Brandy : Listen, young man, and listen very carefully. You don't speak to a General of the Bharatian army in that tone. At least no one speaks to General Brandy like that. The last man who attempted to do so was stripped and hung upside down till he screamed for mercy. One of your friends from the Blitz Krieg or Blitz War Group, I believe. But we didn't forgive him, did we, Colonel M?

C. Mossambi : (smiling) No, sir, we didn't.

Ruby : You bastards! You . . .

G. Brandy : (raising his eyebrows) Again?! This is most distressing. I shall have to order a firing it appears. There'll be a dreadful racket for about ten minutes, but after that you'll all be as quiet as mice. (menacingly) Do you want that to happen?

The murmuring in the crowd has increased at the scarcely veiled threat; and people appear to be wondering what to do. Ruby raises his hand to quell the murmuring.

Ruby : (addresses the gathering) Friends, those of you who wish to leave may do so now. I, for one, will not desert my fellow Blitz being tortured inside.

The crowd appears to hesitate.

G. Brandy : They are not being tortured, you fool. They are being operated upon.

John : Many have DIED! One can smell their rotting corpses. Do you deny that?

G. Brandy : Oh, another one who dares to speak. This

is getting worse. (Addresses John) Obviously, young fool, if several thousand operations are carried out, there may be a few hundred causalities . . . but I see that you have ALL decided to become causalities as well. Or so it appears.

C. Mossambi : Shall I order the troops to fire, sir?

G. Brandy : No, wait. Have you got some cotton wool Mossambi?

C. Mossambi : No, sir.

G. Brandy : Go and get some from the Surgeon. I don't want to hear the firing. My headache may get worse

Col. Mossambi walks down towards the operation theatre site, where the surgeon is still busy performing operations, speaks to the nurse, and collects some cotton wool from her.

C. Mossambi : (eagerly) Now, Sir, shall I order them to fire? Now, sir?

G. Brandy : (stuffing the cotton wool into his ears) Yes, but make sure you instruct them that they must shoot not to injure, but to kill. I don't want to hear a sound aftei ten minutes. If there are injured people, they will be scraming . . . and then my poor nerves. Even this cotton wool won't help me.

Ruby : You will suffer for this, General Brandy. You will suffer. History will not forgive you for what you have done to the people of Blighty.

C. Mossambi : Shall I order, sir?

G. Brandy : Yes.

C. Mossambi : FIRE!!

The firing commences for about two, or three minutes.

Ruby : (shouts) Blitz Kreig!

Chorus : Up, up!!

John	:	Jesus Christ, Jesus Christ!
Chorus	:	Long live, long live!!
Ruby	:	Jesus Christ, Jesus Christ!
Chorus	:	Long live, long live!!

The firing ends. The injured begin moaning. There is more firing. All is quiet then. General Brandy removes the cotton wool from his ears and walks away.

Curtain

Scene 10

Birchbill's house in the South of Blighty. Six weeks have elapsed since Birchbill left for Maha Bharat and two weeks since the massacre took place at Tundun. Behru has called off the sterilization programme. There are masses of Blitz on the streets. Clementine is having a conversation with her friend Lady Mohabattein. It is morning time.

Clementine : (pouring tea) . . . as I was telling you, my dear, Birchie's cable which arrived an hour ago says he will continue to remain in Indra Prastha for a little while longer.

Lady Mohabattein : But Is That Wise My Dear. It's the wrong time for dear Birchbill to be out of the country. There are masses of Blitz on the streets. It's been quite an explosive situation for the past two weeks.

Clementine : Yes, that horrible Tundun massacre, and the killings of Ruby and John in particular. The whole of Blighty is in turmoil, Lady Mohabattein.

Lady Mohabattein : My husband Lord Mohabattein was saying only last night that the time has come for all of us titled Lords and Ladies to return our titles. It's so shameful to keep them when the Generals from Maha Bharat perpetuate such atrocities on our people.

Clementine : Birchie says however that the people must desist from any violence.

Lady Mohabattein : I somehow don't think that's possible, especially since the Enquiry Committee appointed by Prime Minister Behru against General Brandy and Col. Mossambi has completely exonerated them both.

Clementine : What you say was quite true, my dear, but no longer so. The situation till yesterday was that it wouldn't have been possible for the Blitz people to remain silent anymore, but now because of Mungojerrie[23], it may be possible for them to hold their peace.

Lady Mohabattein : Who is Mungojerrie?

Clementine : It's the name of the cat. There was some disagreement for sometime as to whether it was Mungojerrie or Rumpleteazer but finally the matter has been settled by the initial M on the cat's collar that has been found. I think from now onwards Blitz people all over the country are going to start naming their cats Mungojerrie.

Lady Mohabattein : I can't make out head or tail of what you're saying, my dear. What has happened? What did this cat do?

Clementine : Oh, haven't you *heard* what happened last night, my dear.

Lady Mohabattein : I haven't heard, my dear, I keep telling you. Tell, tell, what happened?

Clementine : Well, I get all the latest news even when Birchbill is not around, since the

---

23. Name taken from TS Eliot's 'Old Possum's Book of Practical Cats.'

party sends it anyway, because of course when he is here he must be the first person to be informed of everything. Last night a White revolutionary from the Blitz Kreig disguised himself as a Gypsy and wearing a tattered cloak and shawl went to meet General Brandy. He was let inside the palace where the General lives - where our own King lived till he was beheaded in the Battle of Lassi - because the General has given out standing instructions that Gypsies are to be searched for weapons carefully but allowed inside since they always have something amusing to show. Anyhow, when the revolutionary was admitted into the General's study, he told him, 'Sire, I have brought a present for you because of your many kindnesses to our people,' and the General, who, as you know is always greedy for presents replied 'What is it, man?'. 'Sire, it is a billy,' he said. 'Billy? What's a fucking billy?' said the General. 'Sire,' he said, revealing the animal kept underneath the shawl, 'it is what the famous Blitz cat is called in the colloquial Gypsy tongue.' It was Mungojerrie, of course, a beautiful tabby cat with the most exotic orange and black fur. The General accepted it with alacrity, and ordered his guards to escort the revolutionary till the gates of the palace, but before that to give him two bottles of the finest Bharatian *thara*.[24]

24. A low cost alcoholic beverage

Lady Mohabattein : (all agog) Then? What did Mungojerrie do?

Clementine : The cat was very quiet and well behaved for the next three days and the General became very fond of it. As you know, General Brandy loves flying these newly invented Bindian war planes, even though they say he's very careless and doesn't even hold a pilots license. Last evening he went up for a test-drive in a newly developed two-seater aircraft and he took Mungojerrie along with him to show her the view. Well, Mungojerrie had just been biding her time and lay quite peacefully in the General's unsuspecting lap, when all of a sudden at a moment when the General has his full concentration on the control panels of the aircraft, without any previous warning, she let out a blood curling meow . . . and bit off the General's penis.

Lady Mohabattein : (astonished) Bit off his penis! You don't say?!

Clementine : (well pleased with having succeeded in shocking her friend) Yes, yes, that's what happened. She was actually very fond of eating penises, this particular cat

Lady Mohabattein : Really?!

Clementine : Must have been a feminist in her previous life.

Lady Mohabattein : Or a whore.

Clementine : Perhaps. Anyhow, I believe that the revolutionaries had been training her for years, you see. I believe she'd bitten off many penises before the General's.

Lady Mohabattein : What happened to the General?

Clementine : Oh, the aircraft crashed as the General lost complete control. They had to spend hours collecting the pieces of his body from the wreckage. It was quite clear from a post-mortem report that this is what had happened. So you see my dear, the Enquiry Committee may have exonerated him but nevertheless retribution finally caught up with him. *Divine* retribution, I should call it. As we say in Blighty, if you sow the wind, you will reap the whirlwind and that is how it very clearly happened in the case of General Brandy. Finally, it was a cat, a very ordinary Blitz cat, which twisted the tail of the great Bharatian lion.

Lady Mohabattein : And Mungojerrie?

Clementine : He died too. Poor, valiant cat gave his life in the line of duty. I believe that now the Blitz people will be fonder than ever of their cats. There is a proposal already from some Cat Lovers Society that we should erect a memorial for Mungojerrie, and the tabby cat be declared the national animal of Blighty as and when we achieve independence.

Lady Mohabattein : Now I understand what you were saying earlier. So, Birchbill feels the situation will improve with the death of the General.

Clementine : Yes, he has his pulse on the feelings of the people as you know, and he feels that the Blitz people's feelings will have been somewhat assuaged by this development, as unlike the

Bharatians we are basically not a violent sort of people.

Lady Mohabattein : This is extraordinary news!!

Clementine : It'll be front page news in all the papers tomorrow.

Lady Mohabattein : Yes, I can see the headlines. 'Blighty cat liquidates Bharatian General.'

Clementine : (laughs heartily) Isn't it funny? I think Birchie's right. This incident will placate people somewhat despite what the Blitz Krieg says or does - they try to say that Birchbill is delaying our independence because of his moderation - But of course that's just nonsense. The other important reason why people will calm down is owing to the presence of Mr Behru.

Lady Mohabattein : That's why JP must have sent him in the first place.

Clementine : That's possible. I know Mr Behru is doing everything in his powers to assuage the feelings of our people. Birchie told me to take real good care of him if he drops by. I've received information that, now that things have cooled down a bit in Tundun - after yesterdays incident - he is likely to be coming to Blackpool today itself, and he is sure to drop by in that case.

Lady Mohabattein : (excited) Oh, really! How exciting!

Clementine : Oh, yes, he drops by whenever he is in town. He's very fond of Birchy.

Lady Mohabattein : (cleverly) And no less fond of you too, my dear.

Clementine : (blushes) Oh, please do not tease me, Mohabattein. (is quiet for a moment as if savoring some pleasant memory)

He does know how to pay a lady the most extravagant and beautiful compliments though, I grant you that.

Lady Mohabattein : Oh, my dear, he seems so SINCERE! If he pays you compliments, I'm sure he means them. Now what exactly did he say?

Clementine : (blushes once again) I really can't bring myself to repeat them, my dear.

Lady Mohabattein : (pretending to be hurt) Come ON, my dear. You can trust me, you know.

Clementine : I'll tell you EVERYTHING the next time you come, my dear. I promise you that.

Lady Mohabattein : You know you can pay him compliments back my dear if you like. Isn't he himself so very good looking, besides being such a charming man? By the way, how are things between you and Winston?

Clementine : (a trifle wearily) Oh, all right, I suppose.

Lady Mohabattein : No, I mean . . . did you? . . . as we had planned . . . before he left.

Clementine : (sadly) No, my dear, we didn't. Winston has said he won't have sex till he makes his beloved Blighty free of Bharatian rule. Now what's a girl to do about THAT!

Lady Mohabattein : (sympathetically) Nothing at all, my dear. . . in any case . . . he is so fat ... I mean . . . it can't be at all pleasurable . . . . And my dear . . . there are always ways you know.

The bell rings.

Enter Behru

Behru : (bowing) Good evening, ladies.

Clementine : (rising) Good evening to you, Prime Minister. Please do come in. (introduces LADY M) This is my good friend, Lady . . .

Behru : (kisses the hand) Mohabattein

Lady Mohabattein : (flustered, and visibly flattered) (in a wondering tone) How do you know?

Behru : Oh, Clementine has often spoken of you.

Lady Mohabattein : I'm honored and flattered that you should remember it, Prime Minister.

Behru : Please don't call me Prime Minister. It sounds so formal. After all don't I call you ladies by your first names? This is all Clementine's doing. Sometimes I think you do it deliberately, my dear Clementine, in order to embarrass me.

Clementine : Not at all, my dear Behru. How can you think that?

Lady Mohabattein : Well, I think I'd better be getting along.

Behru : *Please.* I didn't mean to disturb your conversation.

Clementine : What's the hurry, my dear? Do stay with us for a while.

Lady Mohabattein : No, I really have to go. I've just remembered some important business. Please do excuse me.

Exit Lady Mohabattein

Clementine : So, Prime Minister.

Behru : *Please,* Clementine. Don't call me *that.* I will have to perforce believe that you try to embarrass me.

Clementine : (guilelessly) With what motive?

Behru : Well, perhaps because I am the representative of a colonial power.

Clementine : And I am your slave.

Behru : There you go again. Why must you torture me in this fashion?

Clementine : (archly) Then what would you have me do, my dear. (turns her face towards the audience) Shower you with kisses!

Behru : It is not you, but I who am your slave.

Clementine : Prove it.

Behru : (confused) How?

Clementine : By doing as you are bidden.

Behru : I await your commands, Highness.

Clementine : Let JP not hear you say that. He'll accuse you of divided loyalties.

Behru : (patiently) I'm still waiting.

Clementine : For what?

Behru : Orders.

Clementine : Orders?! (laughs) Right. Well . . . kiss me first.

Behru kisses Clementine.

Clementine : That was nice. (smiles) Now once more.

Behru kisses Clementine once more.

Clementine : (eyes closed, an ecstatic smile hovers on her lips) That was even better. (purses her lips anxiously) One of the servants may come in suddenly. I

		think . . . we might adjourn to the bedroom for a while.
Behru	:	Gladly.
Clementine	:	Birchy did say I should take full care of you.

Curtain

Scene 11

The same setting as in Scene 2 (somewhat changed though) . Princess Ujala is sitting on the Peacock Throne at a slightly raised platform and besides her is her great - uncle and advisor Sanjay. At the end of Scene 2 there was (or put it in now) some lightning / thunder, some crackling sounds and a darkening of the stage with SANJAY's voice speaking in the background (which continues to speak - the last sentence at any rate) which ends this scene and opens Scene 3. Now this scene opens in semi darkness with first Clementine's last (tape recorded) words coming on the stage (to maintain the continuity)

Clementine : (only the voice can be heard) Birchy did say that I should take full care of you.

Sutradhaar's Voice In The Background (Sanjay) And so my dearest princess you have just had this glimpse, or rather vision of the past, and it will have to do for the present, even if you crave more, for too much of it cannot be digested by ordinary human beings in one sitting . . . besides it could lead to an addiction of sorts - so back to the present!!

There is the sound of thunder, some lightning crackles and gradually the stage lightens.

Princess U : Damn. The scene had to finish there, did it? (Just when things were beginning to get exciting.)

Sanjay : It's good that it's over, Princess. (looks at his watch) In any case my dear since the contest is scheduled for tomorrow morning, or at noon to be more precise, hadn't you better give some thought at to what the great contest between your two suitors must take place. My suggestion is that you simply cancel the contest, and declare Prince Chanakaya chosen.

Princess U : And Prince Socrates? Could I as well not declare him chosen?

Sanjay : Come on, my dear. Be sensible.

Princess U : No, no *chacha,* the contest must take place. As a matter of fact I have already decided on the test I wish to set them.

Sanjay : Which is? Come tell Uncle.

Enter Footman

Footman : Sire, the Chief of the Maha Bharatian Armed Forces is here to see Her Highness.

Sanjay : Tell him she is very tired and will see him tomorrow in the evening.

Footman : Very good, Sir.

Princess : No, no wait, Footman. Uncle, he could not have come casually at this hour. Footman, go and ask him what is it he wishes to see me about.

Footman : Yes, Your Highness.

Footman goes out briefly, and returns shortly.

Footman : Your Highness, he wishes to confer with you on a matter of national importance. He says the matter is so grave, that is cannot possibly wait. He must see you today itself, preferably now.

Princess : All right, please escort him to my office, and ask him to wait there. I will be there shortly.

Sanjay : But my dear, hadn't you better rest . . .

Princess : No, Great Uncle, if the Commander says

the matter is urgent it must necessarily be the case. (shouts) Anida.

Maid In Waiting : Yes, ma'am

Princess : Go get me my cloak, and the royal seal. It is kept somewhere in the upper bedroom. It may be that it is needed. Some urgent proclamations or orders may need to be issued. Chachaji, you're looking so tired. Hadn't you better get some rest as well.

Sanjay : Yes my dear.

Scene 12

The set is the same as that in the previous scene. However while in the previous scene Princess Ujala was seated in the main hall below (though at a slight elevation) her throne has now been shifted to the top of the staircase. She is dressed resplendently in a *saree* with gold and green colors that are the two colors of the national flag of Maha Bharat, and her jeweled tiara is sparkling. Seated right next to her is her great uncle Sanjay, and at a little distance away is seated a tall statuesque dhoti clad individual. In the main hall below directly opposite the staircase are placed two smaller thrones on which will be seated the two contestants.

Enter Footman

Footman : Your Highness, the members of your cabinet have arrived, together with General Chaudhury.

Princess : Let them in. Let them all be comfortably seated to watch the contest.

Enter General Chaudhury, The Army Commander together with MR GUNDU, MR DANG, MR SHOBHRAJ the senior members of the Princess's Cabinet. Each one bows to the Princess, and is acknowledged by her, before he takes his seat to witness the proceedings that are shortly to ensue.

Re Enter Footman

Footman : Your Highness, the contestants have arrived.

Princess U : Call them in, with due pomp and ceremony.

Footman : (shouts) Prince Socrates!

Enter Socrates

He makes a bow. The Princess with a smile acknowledges his presence.

Footman : (shouts) Prince Chanakaya.

Enter Chanakaya

He makes a bow, gazes searchingly at the Princess and is acknowledged with a smile.

The Princess now descends the staircase Princess Ujala does a dignified *namaste* to each one of them, and then takes him personally in a smiling welcoming fashion to his already earmarked small throne at the foot of the staircase. For a few minutes now the Princess appears to graciously oversee the serving of Sherbet and other dishes to all the guests present, and then she turns towards the entrance.

Princess : Footman, let in all the other important guests, the captains of industry, and leaders of unions, the visiting foreign dignitaries, and chosen members from the ordinary people, so that they too can watch the proceedings. Great Uncle, I leave it to you now to make further announcements.

Sanjay : Yes, yes, of course.

The Princess ascends the staircase and resumes her seat on the peacock throne.

Meanwhile the gate is opened to let in another six men, some of who appeared as princes earlier. They take their seat placed against the rear wall of the hall.

Sanjay : (standing up) The contest will commence shortly. Ladies and Gentlemen, all of you who are gathered here today, it is my duty and indeed my privilege to introduce to you the two contestants who both seek the hand of our Princess. Seated on my left (makes a gesture with his hands) is Prince Chanakaya, the Prince of Patliputra , one of the oldest principalities in Maha Bharat. As every child knows, Maha Bharat is divided into thirty principalities. The ruling prince is almost always a direct descendant of the original King of that region who, five hundred years ago, would have acknowledged the overall suzerainty of the Limshumdin Emperor, Karan Karim. Ever since that time all Princes, though rulers in their own right with a fair measure of autonomy, nevertheless acknowledge the overlordship of the Emperor of Maha Bharat, currently the Empress, or Princess as we are used to calling her fondly on account of her youth and beauty.

The winner in today's contest shall be entitled to marry the Princess and shall be her partner for life. Our Princess shall however continue to rule as the Empress and Monarch Absolute and it shall only be the offspring conceived as a result of this Union who shall be the future Emperor, or Empress of Maha Bharat. I mention this only for the information of some visiting foreign dignitaries who are present in the audience today. Let it also be clarified that the rules of such a contest are clear. Despite having called for a contest, the Princess is not obliged to choose the winner. It may be something, some quality about the loser that impresses her more . . . and therefore I will advise the loser to be gracious. It is possible he might yet be the winner.

The Princess herself without any suggestion from any quarter has in fact decided upon today's contest, which of course though not strictly required, in fitting in the circumstances.

It is now time for me to introduce to all of you the gentleman sitting to my extreme right. This is Shri Shabdgamini, without whom today's contest would not be possible at all.

Shri Shabdgamini (that is not his real name of course), learned academic and scholar, holder of five doctorates, has been outside the country for several years now and for that reason only you may not have heard of him. For the past twenty years he has been busy in establishing Bhartian Universities and Institutes of Higher Learning in some of our overseas dominions in the continent of Europe and elsewhere.

Apart from his erudition and great learning, Mr Shabdgamini has one extraordinary talent, and this special talent is his ability to speak many languages.

All of us assembled here know that we have in the sub-continent of Maha Bharat. twenty seven developed languages which the common people speak and understand and which we teach in our various schools and universities in the various principalities. The most important language is of course the Prustian language for it is the Court language and language of State – the language in which I am presently addressing you - which came into being as a result of efforts by the Great Limshumdin Emperor Karan Karim to create a common language which would nevertheless have the strains and influences of the various tongues spoken in the land.

Apart from Prustian, there remains for the ordinary Bharatian – unless he happens to be Prustian - his mother tongue that is the language of the region he hails from. Many of us gathered here today speak Prustian but in addition we all also know at least one other language that is our mother tongue. Some of us know Bharatian languages apart from these two. I myself can speak three languages.

Prince Socrates seated to my left is by race and birth not a Bharatian yet he can speak apart from his own language, five Bharatian tongues.

(At this announcement there is some clapping from the audience)

I must add that in this respect the achievements of the other prince, Prince Chanakaya, seated to my right are equally singular. Apart from being a scholar, a warrior and a sportsman Prince Chanakaya can speak twelve Bhartian languages.

(At this announcement there is further clapping from the audience)

The Princess herself loves her land so much that she has troubled herself to learn thirteen languages. That is why she is no ordinary Princess. She is the Princess of our hearts.

(Unrestrained clapping follows this announcement)

And this gentleman seated right next to us, Mr Shabdgamini, who is apart from much else a Professor of Linguistics, can speak all, yes *all* the twenty-seven languages as well as a few tongues spoken in our overseas dominions. I leave the floor now to him to tell you about today's contest and to address you, as he will.

Shabdgamini : (standing up) Ladies and Gentlemen, I am not worthy of the praise that has been showered upon me, but yes, it is true, I can speak all the 26 regional languages of Maha Bharat, which taken in conjunction with Prustian adds up to a total of 27 languages. You are aware that Prustian in which I address you is an artificial language created by the collective effort of trained linguists from the different regions of this great land of ours.

We all do however have a mother tongue as well. When a person speaks a language other than his mother tongue he often speaks in an accented fashion. It is possible for someone whose mother tongue it actually is to spot the accent and identify the region the person hails from. However with practice or rigorous training it is possible to eliminate that accent.

I could in today's contest speak all the twenty six languages, and ask you to spot which of these was my mother tongue, but I will proceed somewhat differently.

Firstly, I will not speak but I will recite verse. Great Uncle Sanjay did mention that I have been conferred with five doctoral degrees. One of the doctorates I have earned has been in Classical Bharatian Literature . . . but fear not, I will not bore you with classical verse from the twenty-six different tongues. I will instead recite to you verse that has become very popular with our masses in the various regions.

I could recite twenty-six poems in each of the different

languages at one stretch, but I am afraid it will tire me out, and also it may then take longer than is necessary. By the time I finish it will be evening. What I will do instead is to recite a single poem and then there will be a break for ten minutes. Should a Prince venture to guess on the basis of the poem what language is my mother tongue the contest will be over. If however after a poem, it is not possible for either of the two Princes to say which is my mother tongue then after the break I will recite another poem for them, and so on and forth.

So here goes. The first poem I will recite for you is from ...

Prince Chanakaya : (stands up suddenly) I would like to make a statement concerning the mother tongue of Mr Shabdgamini.

There is an excited buzz in the audience.

Shabdgamini : (raises his eyebrows) A statement? So early in the day? Is it just from my ordinary conversational speech in Prustian that you have already deduced my mother tongue?

Prince Chanakaya : No, not from your speech.

Princess Ujala : Go ahead with your statement, Prince Chanakaya. This is most interesting. A statement at the very beginning.

Prince Chanakaya : It is not the answer, Princess, but it would be close.

Princess Ujala : Go ahead, Prince. We will tell you if it has been close enough or rather good enough.

Prince Chanakaya : I have traveled all over the land to even the most remote parts of our country. There is little about our customs and practices that I am not aware of. When Shabdgamini stood up, and put his hand on the dais, I noticed that he was wearing a gold ring on his little finger, which has a blue pearl studded in it.

(At this comment, Shabdgamini's face breaks into smiles. He nods his head energetically.)

Princess Ujala : Yes, but what does this have to do with the language he speaks.

Prince Chanakaya : Princess, there is a religious custom amongst a certain caste in Bongiligili that the eldest son will wear a gold ring with a blue pearl on his little finger. I know of no other community in the mainland who has follows such a practice.

Princess Ujala : (excitedly) Ah, so you say Shabdgamini's language is Bongiligili. Is that it?

Prince Chanakaya : No other community on the mainland, Princess. However oddly enough there is a community in one of the islands off the east coast of Maha Bharat where I found an identical custom prevails. There too the eldest son wears a gold ring studded with a blue pearl, and also on his little finger. Yet the language they speak is closest to Tellglue. My statement therefore is – it could be the one or the other. Either Bongiligili or Tellglue. The linguist's mother tongue can be no third language.

Princess Ujala : (turns to Shabdgamini) Tell me, is this true that it is indeed one of these tongues.

(Shabdgamini nods his head silently)

Princess Ujala : Let me think for a while.

For a few minutes the Princess is lost in thought. The audience in the hall waits in suspense.

Princess Ujala : (speaking slowly) You have come close, Prince Chanakaya, but not close

		enough, I am afraid. I am of course highly impressed, and will bear your statement in mind, the fact that you have narrowed down the search to only two languages, but I regret the contest is not over yet.

Prince Chanakaya bows his head gracefully.

Princess Ujala	:	Shabdgamini, please continue.
Shabdgamini	:	You have already heard me speak Prustian in conversation, but declamation is different. Accents come out more sharply there. I will therefore begin with a poem in Prustian itself.

(there is clapping from the audience)

This poem is well known throughout Maha Bharat, but is particularly famous in the East as well as our overseas dominions further on in that direction.[25] I invite the participants to guess my accent.

(commences recital)

Thou hast made me endless, such is thy pleasure. This frail vessel thou emptiest again and again, and fillest it ever with fresh life.

This little flute of a reed thou hast carried over hills and dales, and hast breathed through it melodies eternally new.

At the immortal touch of thy hands my little heart loses its limits in joy and gives birth to utterance ineffable.

Thy infinite gifts come to me only on these very small hands of mine. Ages pass, and still thou pourest, and still there is room to fill.

When thou commandest me to sing, it seems that my heart would break with pride; and I look to thy face, and tears come to my eyes.

All that is harsh and dissonant in my life melts into one

25. This poem is taken from Tagore's Gitanjali.

sweet harmony — and my adoration spreads wings like a glad bird on its flight across the sea.

I know thou takest pleasure in my singing. I know that only as a singer I come before thy presence.

I touch by the edge of the far-spreading wings of my song thy feet which I could never aspire to reach.

Drunk with the joy of singing I forget myself and call thee friend who art my lord.

I know not how thou singest, my master! I ever listen in silent amazement.

The light of thy music illumines the world. The life breath of thy music runs from sky to sky. The holy stream of thy music breaks through all stony obstacles and rushes on.

My heart longs to join in thy song, but vainly struggles for a voice. I would speak, but speech breaks not into song, and I cry out baffled. Ah, thou hast made my heart captive in the endless meshes of thy music, my master!

Life of my life, I shall ever try to keep my body pure, knowing that thy living touch is upon all my limbs.

I shall ever try to keep all untruths out from my fingers, knowing that thou art that truth which has kindled the light of reason in my mind.

I shall ever try to drive all evils away from my heart and keep my love in flower, knowing that thou hast thy seat in the inmost shrine of my heart.

And it shall be my endeavor to reveal thee in my actions, knowing it is thy power gives me strength to act.

I ask for a moment's indulgence to sit by thy side. The works that I have in hand I will finish afterwards.

Away from the sight of thy face, my heart knows neither rest nor respite, and my work becomes an endless toil in a shoreless sea of toil.

Today the summer has come at my window with its sighs and murmurs; and the bees are plying their minstrelsy at the court of the flowering grove.

Now it is time to sit quiet, face to face with thee, and to

sing dedication of life in this silent and overflowing leisure.

Pluck this little flower and take it, delay not!! I fear lest it droop and drop into the dust.

I may not find a place in thy garland, but honor it with a touch of pain from thy hand and pluck it. I fear lest the day end before I am aware, and the time of offering go by.

Though its color be not deep and its smell be faint, use this flower in thy service and pluck it while there is time.

My song has put off her adornments. She has no pride of dress and decoration. Ornaments would mar our union; they would come between thee and me; their jingling would drown thy whispers.

My poet's vanity dies in shame before thy sight. O master poet, I have sat down at thy feet. Only let me make my life simple and straight, like a flute of reed for thee to fill with music.'

(loud clapping from the audience as he finishes)

Princess : Now there will be a short recess. Please do come down Mr Shabdgamini, for some refreshment. Your throat is in need of some refreshment, I'm certain.

The Princess, Shabdgamini and Great Uncle Sanjay all three descend the staircase, the one behind the other.

At the same time we see Prince Socrates leaving his throne instead of moving towards the refreshments ascending the staircase at the same time, he bows to the Princess as he crosses her, she looks at him with curiosity, and when the Prince nears Shabdgamini he suddenly puts his leg out and trips him.

Shabdgamini : (as he falls) What the devil! You, you!! *Shala!!!*[26]

Socrates : (helps Shabdgamini up) Forgive me, dear Professor. My sincerest apologies (pauses and turns to the audience

---

26. 'Shala' translates into brother in law, and is a subtle kind of abuse in Bengali. It implies though does not say so directly, that the abuser has made love to the sister of the abused.

which is now looking up, including the Princess) It is my belief that no matter how many languages one may know, the spontaneous expression of one's deepest emotions is inevitably in the mother tongue. Fortunately, I do not know the meaning of that abuse, and will therefore not take any offence, but I do know which language it comes from. Your mother tongue is therefore undoubtedly Bongiligili

Shabdgamini : (nods his head) This is true!

Princess : (turns around smiling and claps) Brilliant, Prince Socrates! Simply brilliant!!

(The audience gathered in the hall all start to clap loudly. Prince Chanakaya looks subdued and sad.

Suddenly the three soldiers posted near the entrance now all stand up.)

First Soldier : Such a choice shall not be permitted!

Second Soldier : Death to the White Prince!

Third Soldier : In the name of Kabir the Great Mystic!

First Soldier : And in the name of Karan Karim the Great Limshumdin!

Second Soldier : Death to the White Prince!

General Chaudhury : (standing up) Drop your swords, soldiers. Your army commander commands you. Drop them now!

Defense Minister : (also stands up and unsheathes a small sword) No, they won't General. These soldiers take their orders from me. Now don't try any funny business. Let these soldiers do their duty. Boys, kill the White Prince, and arrest the Princess.

(The three soldiers move towards the White Prince, swords unsheathed)

Prince Chanakaya : (unsheathing his sword) Halt, ye men! Go not a step further. You will have to step over my dead body first, ere you lay your hands upon the White Prince.

First Soldier : Stand aside, Prince Chanakaya, or your life will not be spared.

Second Soldier : Stand aside Prince. It will be a sad day for us to attack a Bharatian Prince, especially one so valorous as you, but our Guruji, the venerable Guruji who resides in the forest, has also spoken out against the union of the Princess with the White Savage.

Third Soldier : It is against all our religious teachings. Step aside, Prince, that we may do our duty.

Prince Chanakaya : Nay, I have sworn to protect the honor of the Princess, and so have both of you, yet you forget your higher duty. No guest of the Princess, be he white, black or brown shall have a hair of his harmed, so long as I, Prince Chanakaya am here. I shall not permit the slaughter of the White Prince to take place in the palace, even though it may have been to my benefit.

The three soldiers are seen to hesitate

Defense Minister : Boys, just kill this stupid Prince Chanakaya, and then go for the White Prince.

(The three soldiers now lock swords with Prince Chanakaya. A duel follows, with Prince Chanakaya defending himself and protecting Prince Socrates single handedly.)

Princess : Soldiers! Soldiers!! Stop this violence this instant! I say to you as your Queen, stop this violence at once! I will not marry the White Prince. Do you hear me? Do you hear?

(The duel between the soldiers and Prince Chanakaya stops momentarily at these words. Prince Chanakaya looks stunned at the Princess's pronouncement.)

Defence Minister : Kill the White Prince and arrest the Princess you fools.

Third Soldier : (hesitates) But sir, Her Highness says . . .

Defence Minister : Do you trust what she says. Kill both the princes, I said, and then arrest the Princess as well. You'll all three be made Generals, I promise you.

(The door bursts open suddenly)

Enter Guruji

Guruji : Alak Niranjan

First Soldier : Guruji has come!

Second Soldier : Guruji!!

Guruji : There shall be no killings here. Does everyone hear? The Princess is our Queen. Our Queen Empress. The Queen of Hearts. The first monarch in the history of Maha Bharat who has felt the sufferings of the needy and the poor . . .

Defence Minister : (snarls) Soldiers! Soldiers! Don't listen to that old fool. You'll all be Generals by tomorrow morning, I promise you.

Guruji : Arrest that man, whoever he is .

(The soldiers hesitate)

Guruji : Arrest him, my young soldiers.

First Soldier : Come, the Guru has spoken.

Second Soldier : Yes, I cannot disobey the Guru.

(They all now gather around Mr Gundu. One of the soldiers takes an iron chain and ties it around Mr Gundu's hands)

Guruji : And now, all of you gathered here, listen very carefully to what your Princess has to say.

Princess : The contest is over, the villain has been trapped and caught, but before I announce to you all the winners of today's contest, let me explain a few things.

(takes a deep breath) Why did I call Prince Socrates to the contest at all? It was of course that his credentials impressed me. Prior to the *swayamvara* many persons tried to dissuade me from letting him participate, but I held fast to my decision, for was he not as qualified as the others. Also, I must admit that I wished to make a symbolic gesture to the people of Blighty, since I knew fully well that such symbolic gestures carry great weight with the common people.

It was a gesture to show the people of Blighty that I, Princess Ujala, the Queen Empress of Maha Bharat, do not regard the White people to be in any way inferior to the Brown race.

I knew that the Blitz follow closely all events that take place in Maha Bharat. Ever since the time I announced that Prince Socrates too would be one of the few princes who would be permitted to press his suit before me, there has been relative peace and quiet in Blighty and in our other overseas dominions as well.

Last night, my Great Uncle Sanjay showed me the terrible sterilization efforts undertaken during the unfortunate reign of my dear father Jahanpanah – God have mercy upon his soul – by his chief officers, General Brandy and Col. Mossambi, and the terrible Tundun massacre that soon followed thereafter. I could not bear to see the past (though I grant you that some of the love scenes were most interesting). I decided there and then that I would not permit, anymore, during the course of my reign, such bloodshed and repression to take place anymore.

And so I decided that no matter what the results of the contest, the people's fortunes would change and soon after the contest, I would issue a declaration that ensured this.

Were Prince Chankaya to win, I would announce that on account of the intelligent and impressive participation of the White Prince, and in deference to the wishes of the people of Blighty, as a royal gesture the people of Blighty would be henceforth independent and entitled to choose their own King. Prince Chanakaya and I would then jointly rule Maha Bharat.

Were the White Prince to win the Declaration would have announced that having been betrothed thus to a White Prince, it would no longer be appropriate or proper for me to exercise full control over his people. This would be an affront to my husband's dignity, his sense of manhood. Accordingly, it would be declared that henceforth the Blitz would have their independence from Bharatian rule, and it would be Prince Socrates, the Prince who never surrendered, who would be the Ruler and Monarch Absolute over Blighty as well as over our other western dominions, wherein the White people resided.

All this planning of mine came to naught yesterday, because of a few developments that took place after watching the events of the past with my Uncle Sanjay.

In the evening I heard the people marching on the streets and calling for the White Prince to return to his land. They were chanting slogans against him, whereas it was only at my instance that he was able to visit Maha Bharat and be a suitor at the *swayamvara*. Nonetheless the protest march did make an impression on me.

Then yesterday, when the Commander of my Armed Forces, General Chaudhury, came to my palace at night, I knew that something serious was amiss. He told me that he had received reliable information from some quarters that there would be an attempt to assassinate Prince Socrates during the contest today.

What would happen were such an attempt to succeed? It is not so difficult to guess.

There would have commenced agitations against the Empire of Maha Bharat all over Blighty. The Blitz people would not lie quiet about this. It would immediately be felt by the people that possibly I myself had had a hand in the assassination, for I wished to eliminate a possible future leader of theirs.

And the consequences of these mass agitations? More repression by the Bhartian forces, more shelling of poor people's homes, more killings of the innocent.

Guruji too came to visit me last night. He told me very frankly that the people of Maha Bharat would not accept a White Prince as my husband. He said he was a religious person, not at all interested in power politics, but he wished that the wishes of the people were not ignored, and I believed him. He said were I to choose the White Prince, he would be forced to oppose me tooth and nail. He had already in fact issued a statement to the effect that he was opposed to a union between the White Prince and me. Then he said something that went beyond the assassination attempt mentioned by the General. He said he had received word of an attempt to assassinate the White Prince, and also to have me arrested. An attempt to topple the dynasty!

That got me thinking. First General Chaudhury and then the Guruji saying the same thing more or less. There were only three people powerful enough in Government to even think of toppling the dynasty. Their only possible excuse which could find acceptance with the people could be that I Princess Ujala, the Queen Empress, had chosen a white suitor to be her future husband in the presence of this august audience. For that person's plan to succeed it was crucially important that Prince Socrates win the contest. Were he to attempt a coup in the absence of this possibility, the people would certainly rise up against him.

After Guruji spoke to me yesterday, after careful thought and deep meditation, I gave him my solemn assurance that in deference to his wishes, and those of the people (and also in terms of my own desires I believe) I would give my consent to marry only Prince Chanakaya.

At the same time I informed him that I wished the contest to proceed, for it would be an opportunity in which the plot to assassinate the White Prince and overthrow the royal dynasty could well be unearthed. I told the Guruji that I was setting a contest which Prince Chanakaya could not possibly win, and which Prince Chanakaya was bound to win. In any event, even if Prince Socrates did somehow succeed, as he has done, I could still exercise my royal prerogative of choosing the loser.

Accordingly, since I wanted Prince Chanakaya to win, last night I asked Shabdgamini to wear his traditional ring with the blue pearl. It would be a sure giveaway I felt. While Shabdgamini's accents were impeccable, Prince Chanakaya would spot the ring on his finger. He is from Patliputra where there is trade in the blue pearl and everyone knows it is found in the Bay of Bengal. He would also know that it carries a religious significance for the Bongs, who all according to the religious tradition wear this ring on their little finger, which was the case with our linguist professor as well.

I was certain that Prince Chanakaya would guess immediately, being a scholar as well as a warrior who has traveled to all the distant parts of the land. What I did not realize was that the Prince has traveled so far and wide, that he has come across another island in the Bhartian Ocean, where the blue pearl is also found and the very same custom prevails. The people however speak another tongue, Oriya. As he informs us a thousand years ago these people migrated from Oriyaland, but somewhere in the migration picked up the Bong custom, though not the language.

While the contest was on, and Shabdgamini was singing his songs, I kept gazing at the faces of the three senior cabinet ministers and tried to make out which of the three was the guilty party, but there faces gave nothing away. They could all be together in this too', I pondered.

At the crucial moment, when Prince Socrates tripped Shabdgamini, I saw my chance to bring the monster out of the closet. 'Brilliant, Prince Socrates!' I shouted, and in a trice the villain had shown his true face and was shouting commands.

The result. You know it already, but let me say it again. It would have been the same even without the intervention of Guruji. It is not that Prince Socrates has impressed me any the less, but I am simply overwhelmed by Prince Chanakaya's valor, integrity and spirit of self-sacrifice, not to say deep knowledge of our land and its ways.

I must add here that perhaps much more groundwork needs

to be established before the different races of our planet – races created equal by Lord Almighty – can begin to marry and beget children. Perhaps after another fifty years, such marriages between people from different races will become more acceptable, and in a hundred years from now they may even become commonplace.

Let there be peace in our land. There has been far too much violence and bloodshed in the past. I have today devised an alternative better by far to the one of two monarchies I had conceived earlier.

And what pray is that? Prince Socrates has answered rightly and with wisdom, but Prince Chanakaya has acted valorously, knowing fully well that the results of his valor might be victory for Prince Socrates and defeat for him. Had he today not intervened to protect the White Prince, I shudder to think what might have happened.

For his courage and nobility, which all of you are a witness to today, I grant to Prince Chanakaya my hand in matrimony...

(There is clapping and cheering from the audience at this announcement)

For his right answer, I grant to Prince Socrates the freedom of his people . . . and the people of Maha Bharat too are made free today. The people shall be free, not under two monarchs, but shall have the freedom to elect the leader of their choice for a period of five years . . . and they may change that choice after the period is over.

(There is some subdued clapping at this announcement)

I, Princess Ujala, having chosen the Prince, Prince Chanakaya as my partner for life shall henceforth lead the life of an ordinary Bharatian woman for the rest of my years. I do hereby . . . abdicate.

Here too henceforth the people shall elect their leader.

(At this announcement there are shouts and cries of "No, Princess, no!' from the audience)

Curtain Falls

Sutradhaar's Voice Comes Over: And so the song of freedom which sprang forth from the lips of our dear, dearest Princess, the most beloved of them all, traveled far and wide and all over the planet old sodden monarchies were abolished, and societies became more liberated and free? Or did they? (pauses) At any rate, the modern foundations of democratic governance were laid.

Scene 13

A brightly lit pub-like restaurant. The entire cast of the play 'CONQUEST AT NOON' is seated inside at various tables. All except Socrates, that is. The Princess is looking young and sexy in a skimpy top and 'hot' pants. A visibly drunk Behru is playing cards (or billiards) with Lord Pearlson. The General is acting as the Bar Tender and is serving drinks. A television set is mounted in the corner of the room.

T V Announcer: The play acts as a powerful reminder to the Bharatian people that a great deal of what was done in the name of Empire, under the name of the 'brown mans burden' was completely unjustified and brutal. No race is superior or inferior and we have learnt - and continue to learn - a great deal from the subjugated white people. This year the play that has received the largest number of nominations happens to be a play precisely on this theme. CONQUEST AT NOON, the play which everyone is talking about has received not six, not seven, not eight, but . . . (a theatrical pause) a total of NINE nominations in different categories from best play, to best actor, best actress, best villain, best comedian, best script and so on and forth. Tonight, in a while from now we will announce the winner of the major awards, and for the rest you will have to watch our live telecast of the Fony awards ceremony tomorrow evening.

Voice In The Background: (not Sanjay's voice) So we come to the last scene of our play, Ladies and Gentlemen. Wasn't there some obscure Blitz poet who said that life itself was a play. In which case our play would be - you guessed it - a play within a play within a play *within* a play, or to put it simply play to the power of three. Anyhow, I leave you with the cast of the play sitting inside a restaurant where they smack their snacks and drink their drinks while awaiting the announcement on television of the Fony Awards of the year. All are present inside, except for Socrates, who at the moment is having an argument with the Gateman, who is not letting him in, despite his brilliant performance, which you Laydas and Gentlewomen, have already seen. Yes, friends, that's the sad truth, which also happens to be the moral of the play, yessir this play has a moral, unfortunate, isn't it, but there it is. I'm merely a voice in the play, a disembodied voice at that, so can't do very much about what the playwright in his wisdom or madness thought fit to do, yes, I'm coming to it, the moral of the play that is, is that despite the high sounding rhetoric and fine emotions displayed in the previous scene, it was only a play you see. Yes, it was based on historical fact, but real life is not made up of people like Princess Ujala. Let me add that real life in some ways is much worse than you have just seen dear audience - and also in some ways better. But let me not rob you of the climax . . . even though I personally had guessed it.

Chanakaya : So as in the play, so too in real life Princess?

Princess : Let's see. I'll tell you after the Fony Awards are announced. They're at ten o'clock, aren't they? Only fifteen minutes left now.

Chanakaya : Maybe they give you the best actress, the General best director, and me best actor.

Princess : (haughtily) Not very likely.

Chanakaya : (petulantly) Why do you say that, Princess? The play has done very well, hasn't it? We ran for fifteen weeks continuous at the Prithvi.[27] That's a record.

Princess : Why don't you go and get me a drink? Fat lot of care you'll show for me. Can't you see the lady's throat is dry?

Chanakaya : Sorry, dear. (standing up) What'll you have?

Princess : Tomato juice.

---

27. Prithvi is Hindustani for Globe or earth. It is in fact one of the important theatre companies in India.

Chanakaya	:	Plain or with some *madira*[28]?
Princess	:	You know I always like *madira* in my Tomato juice. By the way, where's Socrates.
Chanakaya	:	I don't know. I've been wondering myself.
Princess	:	He should have been here you know.
Chanakaya	:	Absolutely! I think he doesn't like to hang about with us. He has some complex.
Princess	:	Whatever gave you this idea?
Chanakaya	:	Well, as you know, I 'm very fond of him…
Princess	:	Are you?
Chanakaya	:	Oh, yes!! I love him very much, but he doesn't like me for some reason.
Princess	:	Oh, that's not true!
Chanakaya	:	Has he ever mentioned it to you?
Princess	:	Mentioned what?
Chanakaya	:	That he likes me.
Princess	:	No, he hasn't but surely that doesn't mean…
Chanakaya	:	And has he ever told you that he likes *you?*
Princess	:	No, he hasn't, but …
Chanakaya	:	No buts, Princess. It's plain and simple. He just doesn't like our company.
Princess	:	Perhaps there is a very good reason why he couldn't make it tonight.
Chanakaya	:	Ask the General. If there *is* any reason, he would know.
Princess	:	I've already asked. Anyhow, never mind. Just get my drink please.
		You know, Chanakaya, Socrates might pip you to the post. He was rather good.
Chanakaya	:	(gruffly) Don't talk sheeeet, lady. Wait, I'll just get you your drink.

28 'madira' is an Indian term for alcohol.

Chanakaya goes across to the Bar, where General pours him a drink. They start having a muted conversation. Meanwhile, outside the restaurant, Socrates is trying to convince the Gateman to let him in.

Gateman : Can't you read the sign board, mate? Or do I have to read it out to you. (reads it aloud) PRIVATE PARTY. UNAUTHORISED PERSONS NOT ALLOWED INSIDE. That clear enough for you.

Socrates : No, it's not clear enough for me, my good man. Don't you recognize me, Gateman? I played the leading role in the play. I'm Socrates, man.

Gateman : 'ow do I know 'at?

Socrates : Didn't you see the play?

Gateman : What play youse is talking about? Do you think people like me can afford to see a play. Pay two hundred rupees for a three-hour show. I could get sucked off for half the price.

Socrates : Well, then, didn't you see my picture in the newspapers

Gateman : I got better things to do than read the papers.

Socrates : Well, my good man, why don't you just call someone from inside and have him recognize me?

Gateman : (craftily) You think you're smart, huh? Mr Chanakaya told me not to disturb anyone inside on any account. It's he who told me to be very sure no unauthorized persons got in.

Socrates : And why do you assume that I am not a respected member of this private party? Did the people who came before me carry invitation cards?

Gateman : No, they didn't.

Socrates : Then why are you singling me out, my good man.

Gateman : That's because Mr Chanakaya said...

Socrates : Yes, what else did he say?

Gateman : He said someone like you would try to get in and disturb the party, and he didn't want that to happen on any account.

Socrates : Someone like me, he said?

Gateman : That's right. He said it would be a tall person with a beard just like yours.

Socrates : Did he say anything else?

Gateman : Well...(hesitates)

Socrates : Did he say it would be a gow?

Gateman : Well, yes my friend, he did say that. I don't mean any offences, but he did say that. And you are one, I can see plainly enough.

Socrates : (grimly) Oh, he did, did he? And what about wogs?

Gateman : (puzzled) Wogs?! What are wogs?

Socrates : Never mind that. Just a new word I have invented. Listen, my friend, do you know what the party inside is all about?

Gateman : Oh, yes. It's Mr Chanakaya's engagement party.

Socrates : (shocked) Mr Chanakaya's engagement party?! What are you saying?

Gateman : Why do you repeat my words? That's what it is. Mr Chanakaya has even ordered some expensive *sherbet* for this occasion.

Socrates : (addresses the audience in an anguished voice) So all the Princess's kind ways meant nothing! (bitterly) And I poor fool imagined those shy glances, those soft expressions, and those kindnesses *meant* something! All the while, she was clear in her mind that it would be Chanakaya whom she would marry. Why, oh why did she play this game with me? Women!!

Socrates : (turns to the gateman) My friend, you are deceived. Today's party is meant to be a gathering of all the participants of the most important theatrical production of the year. There is no engagement ceremony being celebrated. (something occurs to him, and he takes out a pamphlet from his coat pocket). Here, see this! This is a brochure of the play and you will find that everyone at the party has his photo on this page. See, that's Mr Chanakaya, that's the director of the play, that's me. Do you understand?

Gateman : (scratching his head) Well, yes, those are all the people I've let inside, and that's you all right.

Socrates : (angry now) Well, now are you going to let me enter, or do you want to lose your job?

Gateman : (looks at the pictures again, and is satisfied) I must have been misled by the gentleman, Sir. A practical joke perhaps. (in an apologetic tone now) You may go in, Sir.

Enter Socrates

General : (comes across to receive him) Welcome, welcome Socrates! Come in, come in. Where the hell have you been, dear fellow? We've been missing you like anything. The Princess has asked for you ever so often. Our fates are about to be decided. What can I get for you, my dear?

Socrates : Glass of Hemlock, please.

General : Plain or on the rocks.

Socrates : Neat please.

General : One glass of Hemlock coming up. Sit down, Socrates. Sit down, my boy. (calls out) Princess, Chanakaya, come here. Join us. Another five six minutes and the awards will be announced.

Chanakaya : Hi there, Socks. I hope you didn't have a problem getting here.

Socrates : (angrily) Why do you ask? Should I have had a problem?

Princess U : Channy's just being concerned. You don't have to bite his head off.

Socrates : And you it appears are only concerned about dear Channy's feelings

Princess U : You know that's not true. I just try to stop you both from fighting all the time. Why do you fight?

Socrates : Well, if you must know its because . . .

General : Because you both want to win the Fony Award and are afraid the other guy will get it.

Socrates : I was going to say . . .

Chanakaya : Excuse me folks, I'm just going to get myself a drink.

General : Me too. Come, Channi.

They walk off in the general direction of the Bar

Princess : So, Socrates! Happy?

Socrates : (surly) No! I feel I've been used.

Princess : Used? How?

Socrates : Well, just so you Brown people can have a good cry about all the evil things you did to us White people in the past. Things haven't changed really. In the play, the Princess gives all kinds of profound reasons why she chose Chanakaya and not Socrates. It may have been true of the Princess Ujala that she was not color conscious when it came to a marriage decision, but it's not true of others, is it?

Princess : You speak in riddles, White Man. What is it? Out with it?

Socrates : (bitterly) I don't speak in riddles. It's you

whose eyes say one thing, and whose actions say quite another thing.

Princess : What on earth has upset you so, Socrates? I've never known you like this. You are always so calm and controlled.

Socrates : I'm sorry. I have no right...

Princess : Tell me please. You can confide in me. I know I haven't done anything, but perhaps you are angry with all women? Is it your girl friend from Blighty who has said or done something? (slaps her forehead) *Uff* I am sorry. I was not supposed to mention her. Chanakaya vowed me to secrecy. He said it was a secret between him and you.

Socrates : My girlfriend in Blighty? I *have* no girlfriend. In Blighty, or anywhere else.

Princess : (nonplussed) But Channi said...

Socrates : And if I had one, Chanakaya would be the last person on earth, with whom I would share that information. Did he tell you I have a girl friend?

Princess : Yes.

Socrates : I *have* no girl friend, but yes, there *is* a girl I love ... (tears come to his eyes)...but she won't have me.

Princess : Oh, Socrates, don't be so upset. Who is she?

Socrates : She is getting married to someone else.

Princess : To whom?

Socrates : To Chanakaya.

Princess : Who is getting married to Chanakaya?

Socrates : You are.

Princess : I am?

Socrates : Yes, the Gateman told me. And Chanakaya told him. (suddenly struck by a thought) Tell me it isn't true?

Princess : What isn't true?

Socrates : That you have agreed to marry Chanakaya.

Princess : Well, I haven't agreed as yet, but I did tell him I would think it over.

(They are both silent)

Princess : Who is this girl you love?

Socrates : I have to tell you now.

Princess : Yes.

Socrates : It's you, Princess. I love you, and want to marry you.

Princess : (in a wondering tone) Really? Why didn't you say anything then?

Socrates : I don't have a job. I don't have money.

Princess : Oh, that doesn't matter!

Socrates : It *does* matter. If I do have some money tomorrow...will you consider marrying me?

Princess : Yes, I will...consider your proposal.Why are you so late today? We were wondering...

Socrates : I was stuck at the gate for half an hour. The Gateman wouldn't let me in.

Princess : Really?!

Socrates : (angrily) I had to convince him I was invited to the party..

Princess : (shocked) It's not true!!

Socrates : (very calm now) Very true, my dear!! And guess who put him up to it. Our dear friend Chanakaya - who decided to leave just now when he thought there could be some awkward revelations - gave the intructions to him.

Princess : (white faced) Is that so?

Socrates : So it is, Princess. I don't want to badmouth any man, but with Chanakaya I think I've had enough.

Princess : The liar, the actor, pretending he cares for you . . . and all the time I thought it was you who does not return his affection . . . (in a stage whisper) . . . nor mine.

The General and Chanakaya return with their drinks. Chanakaya is visibly tipsy now, having been seen to toss down a couple of drinks at the Bar, while the General's *thandai*[29] is being prepared. Other actors in the play such as Col. Mossambi, and the various princes also come and join the group, now that the awards are soon to be announced.

Chanakaya : Listen, Socrates, don't mind, but I have to say it before the awards, just in case, as the General said, you beat me to it. If you do get the Fony, it won't be because you were better than me. It will be a politically correct gesture on the part of the Academy, that's all.

(There is some laughter)

Princess U : Chee! What a cheapo thing to say!!

Socrates : Listen, you brown bastard ...

General : Hey, cut it out, you guys. It's time for the announcement of the major awards.

Princess : Why do they announce the major awards the day before on television before the actual ceremony?

General : Oh, they found that otherwise the main winners often didn't bother to attend the ceremony. It happened a couple of times like that, and viewers were terribly disappointed so now the major winners are announced a day before

The television screen lightens.

Television Presenter: Ladies and Gentlemen. The announcement you have all been waiting for eagerly. Who are

---

29. A traditional Indian drink with almonds, cashews and quite often opium.

the winners in this years prestigious Fony awards for the best play, best actress, best director, best villain, best comedian and best actor? The winners as determined by the jury, from whom we have heard just a few moments ago are:

Conquest At Noon for best play

Princess For Best Actress In The Play Conquest At Noon

General For Best Director In The Play Conquest At Noon

General For Best Villain In The Play Conquest At Noon

Col Mossambi For Best Comedian In The Play Conquest At Noon

For the award of best actor the Jury found it exceedingly difficult to choose between Chanakaya and Socrates, both of whom secured the nomination of best actor for the same production, another record of a kind. The jury wanted to make a special mention of the fact, that between Socrates and Chanakaya, it was a very close thing with six members of the jury voting for the one and seven for the other. The seven against six vote awarded it to ...

Chanakaya

Everybody claps. SOCRATES's expression is one of dismay

General : (switches the t v off) I guess we can turn off the television set now. It's been a wonderful result. Four Fonys. Best in my career and must be some kind of a record, I'm sure. I'd like to make a small announcement at this point of time. As the t v announcer said the jury found both our lead actors evenly matched in their performance, and I beleive the loser must get something in compensation. I have decided to offer Socrates a junior partnership in the company.

There is an awed silence in the group, for this is an extremely attractive and unprecedented offer by one of the biggest theatre directors in Maha Bharat. Socrates brightens up visibly and it's now Chanakaya's turn to look upset.

Socrates : That's mighty generous of you, General, but you don't have to do this.

General : It's for my own selfish reasons, my dear. I'm too old to run this company on my own. I need a younger more energetic partner to take care of some things, and I would be hard pressed to find someone with your wisdom and judgment. You may recall my having mentioned this to you some months ago.

Socrates : Yes, I do, but I never thought...

General : (with a twinkle in his eye) I 'm sure this will help you with your ladylove, will it not?

Socrates : I'm not so sure about that, Sir, but thank you very much.

Gradually everyone in the group departs and left behind are only Chanakaya, Socrates and the Princess.

Chanakaya : (comes up to the Princess) So sweetheart . . . now that I've won the Fony as had been promised, are you ready to keep your side of the bargain?

Princess : The deal is off. You may have won the Fony - through what dubious means, I do not wish to guess, now that I know you better - but it's Socrates I'm marrying.

Chanakaya : (stunned) What?!

Socrates : What?!

Princess : (hurt) You don't want me?

Socrates : Of course I do, my Princess. More than anything in this world. You said you would consider my proposal, but you said it in such a way I thought you were being polite.

Princess : Just teasing you, honey.

Socrates : (understanding) I was tortured by the thought that there was a third person, in whom you were more interested. Will you always torture me like this?

Princess : Only now and then, my sweetness.

Chanakaya : What about me?!

Socrates : Get lost, you Fony actor. Didn't you hear the princess?

Chanakaya : (bitterly) I'll get you for this. Trying to take my girl away from me.

Princess : He's not trying anymore, Channi. He's *got* me. Stop acting like a loser now. You've won the Fony. Be happy enough with that.

Chanakaya : (shaking his fist) I'll see you both!!

Socrates : Not in the same production again.

Exit Chanakaya

Socrates and the Princess are left alone. The lights grow dim. A romantic song begins playing in the background. They both snuggle up on the sofa and kiss. They break apart.

Socrates : If I'm going to join the company as a junior partner, not only can I then afford to have a wife, but I can make a try at becoming a director, and scriptwriter as well as an actor, just like the General.

Princess : You're going to write a play, Soccy darling. What is this play going to be all about, my genius sweetheart?

Socrates : I have a few ideas. How about a historical fantasy?

Princess : (puzzled) A historical fantasy? You mean a historical play like this one.

Socrates : No. We all know that the Brown race has ruled the world. The General's play is no fantasy, because the story is based on actual historical facts. My script will go much further. (getting excited now) Suppose it had been the other way around. *Suppose, just for one mad, insane moment that it was the White people who got together and colonized the world.*

What would have happened then?

Princess : (wide-eyed) Mmm. What an idea?! It sounds very exciting. Do you think it could work? What will the play be called?

Socrates : I don't know. I have a few titles in mind. Let me see how they grab you. How about this one - FREEDOM AT MIDNIGHT

Princess : (snuggling up) FREEDOM AT MIDNIGHT! Wow! That sounds real sexy-like making wild uninhibited love in the late hours of the night!! (pauses, as if thinking) What on earth does it mean though in the context of your play?.

Socrates : (stroking her face) As you know the Bharatians attacked the city of Tundun at noon, and caught the Blitz off guard because the Blitz soldiers were all too busy sun-bathing. That's why our play is called CONQUEST AT NOON. In this play of mine, the enslaved Brown people will win their freedom at midnight. Is it too bizarre? How does it grab you?

Princess : (strokes his beard) Well... it's an idea. A bit fantastic though, my darling.

Socrates : Well, it sounds good to me. (kisses her)

Socrates : To me too. (kisses him)